Deleuze Studies
Volume 8 Number 3 2014
Deleuze and the Concepts of Cinema

By Daniela Angelucci
Translated by Sarin Marchetti

Edinburgh University Press

This publication is available as a book (ISBN: 9780748697731) or as a single issue or part of a subscription to *Deleuze Studies*, Volume 8 (ISSN: 1750-2241). Please visit www.euppublishing.com/dls for more information.

Subscription rates for 2015

Four issues per year, published in February, May, August and November

		Tier	UK	EUR	RoW	N. America
Institutions	Print & online	1	£133.50	£146.30	£154.90	$263.50
		2	£167.00	£179.80	£188.40	$320.50
		3	£208.50	£221.30	£229.90	$391.00
		4	£250.00	£262.80	£271.40	$461.50
		5	£283.50	£296.30	£304.90	$518.50
	Online	1	£113.50	£113.50	£113.50	$193.00
		2	£142.00	£142.00	£142.00	$241.50
		3	£177.00	£177.00	£177.00	$301.00
		4	£213.00	£213.00	£213.00	$362.00
		5	£241.00	£241.00	£241.00	$409.50
	Additional print volumes		£112.50	£129.70	£138.30	$235.00
	Single issues		£44.00	£50.00	£52.00	$88.50
Individuals	Print		£41.00	£54.00	£62.50	$106.50
	Online		£41.00	£41.00	£41.00	$73.50
	Print & online		£51.50	£64.50	£73.00	$124.00
	Back issues/single copies		£11.00	£14.00	£16.50	$28.00
	Student Print		£24.50	£37.50	£46.00	$78.00
	Student Online		£24.50	£24.50	£24.50	$44.00
	Student Print & online		£31.00	£44.00	£52.50	$89.50

How to order

Subscriptions can be accepted for complete volumes only. Print prices include packing and airmail for subscribers outwith the UK. Volumes back to the year 2000 (where applicable) are included in online prices. Print back volumes will be charged at the current volume subscription rate.

All orders must be accompanied by the correct payment. You can pay by cheque in Pound Sterling or US Dollars, bank transfer, Direct Debit or Credit/Debit Card. The individual rate applies only when a subscription is paid for with a personal cheque, credit card or bank transfer.

To order using the online subscription form, please visit www.euppublishing.com/page/dls/subscribe

Alternatively you may place your order by telephone on +44 (0)131 650 6207, fax on +44 (0)131 662 3286 or email to journals@eup.ed.ac.uk using your Visa or Mastercard credit card. Don't forget to include the expiry date of your card, the security number (three digits on the reverse of the card) and the address that the card is registered to.

Please make your cheque payable to Edinburgh University Press Ltd. Sterling cheques must be drawn on a UK bank account.

If you would like to pay by bank transfer or Direct Debit, contact us at journals@eup.ed.ac.uk and we will provide instructions.

Contents

Acknowledgements

Daniela Angelucci would like to thank Ian Buchanan, Valentina De Filippis and Sarin Marchetti.

This text first appeared as *Deleuze e i concetti del cinema*, Quodlibet, Macerata, 2012.

Cover image

Monir Shahroudy Farmanfarmaian, Recollections II, 2008, Mirror Mosaic and reverse glass painting, 160x100cm - Coutesy of ROSE ISSA PROJECTS. CAB - Contemporary Art Brussels, Exhibition "THE FOLD", 18.04 - 15.06.2013

Deleuze Studies 8.3 (2014): iv
DOI: 10.3366/dls.2014.0149
© Daniela Angelucci
www.euppublishing.com/dls

Deleuze and the Concepts of Cinema

Preface

Daniela Angelucci   University of Roma Tre
Translated by Sarin Marchetti University College Dublin

> Man is the animal who goes to the cinema.
> Giorgio Agamben

The grounding idea of this book is the one expressed in the final pages of Gilles Deleuze's two volumes on cinema, where the author advocates the coincidence between cinematographic art and philosophy. By imagining a divinatory hour – the 'midday-midnight' – during which asking what cinema consists in means at the same time asking what is philosophy, Deleuze commenced a novel way of understanding the relationship between the two practices: the former creating images while the latter invents concepts. In this new scenario, philosophy does not consider films – and perhaps their narrative content alone – as a mere repository of examples used to corroborate its reflections as sometimes happens in the contemporary landscape of the philosophy of cinema, which goes as far as to treat stylistic choices as sheer accessories. According to Deleuze, the bond between cinema and philosophy is rather one of radical analogy, in which it can be said that both deal with the same problems although each one using its own tools and expressive devices.

Now, which form might this relationship take? If, as Deleuze writes in the context of his direct questioning about the very nature of philosophy,

Deleuze Studies 8.3 (2014): 311–313
DOI: 10.3366/dls.2014.0150
© Daniela Angelucci
www.euppublishing.com/dls

'[the philosopher] assumes in advance the goodwill of thinking ... [and] all his investigation is based on "premeditated decisions" ' – that is, if what is necessary to philosophise is the feeling of an urge – this need emerges when the philosopher, rather than commenting on the work of a certain director, feels that they share a certain question or a common cause. This kind of friendship based on the sharing of the same goal, of the same preoccupation, is also the moving reason for Deleuze to engage a certain philosopher (whatever his philosophical tradition) or a certain artist. However, with cinema this encounter seems to take place in a more spontaneous and powerful way than with other artistic expressions, because it originates in a collision – sometimes violent – with images. These images often reveal an 'unexpected disposition' to show the life of the mind as condensed into a vision.

In this sense, the true objects of the theory of cinema are the concepts that cinema generates when understood as a practice of images. In this sense, philosophy alone – when understood as a conceptual practice – is able to 'constitute the concepts of cinema itself', as the last line of *The Time-Image* as well as the very title of this volume read. My journey winds around some of those concepts, ten in all. The book represents in the first place an introduction to Deleuze's reflection on cinema, but aspires at the same time to emphasise some of its aspects over others – trying at once to carefully avoid, as Deleuze himself once claimed, a double reproach: namely, both excessive erudition (which makes the reading complicated and tedious) and exaggerated familiarity (which in venturing to reproduce the style of the author at hand always gives poor results).

This volume envisages an exposition, carried out in the first four chapters, of the fundamental steps of *The Movement-Image* and *The Time-Image* in the wake of Bergson's thought. First, the book presents the issues of cinema that Deleuze labels as classical: namely, the idea of movement as the smallest unit of film, that is the sequence shot (*plan-séquence*), and the articulation of the cinematographic image into perception, action and affection ('Movement'). Second, it reconstructs the emergence of modern cinema: the possibility of rendering the theme of time through images – a theme which, independently from the evolution of the plot, becomes central with the appearance and diffusion of a novel cinematographic style ('Time'). In describing the two eras of cinema I shall focus on the passage to modernity, that is to the moment in which, departing from neorealism and *nouvelle vague*, some philosophical issues such as those of virtuality and falsity seem to act as the real characters of films ('Virtual' and 'Modernity').

The central part of the book represents instead a pause in the constellation of problems originating from the theme of falsity understood as the capacity of art – and of cinema in particular – to progress in always novel and original ways falling outside the question of truth ('Falsehood'). The overcoming of truthfulness and judgement means for Deleuze believing in life as an affirmative force and in an immanent system of values ('Life'); thus conceived, the becoming of a reality gets constituted through a series of acts and inventions similar to the ones of art, which does not imitate, but rather repeats, reality. In the case of the cinematographic device, this is a repetition that is already characterised since its origin as shifting and, paradoxically, as difference ('Repetition'). As regards the issue of falsity as a potentiality of art and of modern cinema, Orson Welles is the director with whom Deleuze shares a common cause. At the origin of this encounter we can situate the thought of Nietzsche, who first inspired the concept of life as a force constantly trying to overcome itself and as faithfulness 'to the Earth and to human beings'. As regards repetition, I will instead investigate a common cause with Freud: this rather difficult task – whose outcomes will be less obvious if compared with the philosophical and cinematographic friendships just suggested – moves from the idea that the passage from the compulsion to repeat to repetition as differential movement can be envisioned already in some Freudian writings.

Finally, I shall offer a reading of some films related to some particular Deleuzian philosophical categories: the line of thought which from repetition as difference leads to the themes of the double and of the simulacrum will be reprised through a film by Raúl Ruiz ('Simulacrum'); in the film *The Most Dangerous Game* by Ernest Schoedsack and Irving Pichel, I will locate a plot, various characters and some places depicted and constructed in a modality which confirms the interpretation, critical as well clinical, of sadism (and masochism) defended by Deleuze in *Coldness and Cruelty* ('Sadism'); a confrontation with Picasso's painting as it is shown at work in the film by Henri-Georges Clouzot will represent the occasion to highlight the theme of chance, of involuntariness and of the freedom of hazard in the pictorial processes as well as in art in general ('Chance').

Movement

I.

In the first half of the 1980s, with the two volumes *The Movement-Image* and *The Time-Image*, Gilles Deleuze inaugurated a novel modality of thought on cinema that is radically distant from a simply critical perspective, but also different from an a posteriori reflection on cinema's products. The two texts, fully inscribed in the overall philosophical arch preceding them of which they embrace the theoretical premises, assume as their point of departure the affirmation of a strong analogy between the two practices: the one of cinema and the one of philosophy. Differently from other theories – for example, far removed from the semiotical attempt to grasp the semiotic structures and narrative element of films – Deleuze's theory does not consider the numerous films mentioned in his books as object to be analysed or as aesthetic outcomes to be evaluated, but rather as products of an inventive act analogous to the one taking place in philosophy.

Thus, in order to follow his investigations on the cinematographic image, the theoretical premise that we should be accepting does not regard first and foremost cinema, but rather philosophy itself, which would not be a contemplative, reflective, or communicative activity as it has been often believed, but rather is defined by Deleuze as a 'continuous creation of concepts' in a way analogous to cinema's being a creation of images. And if concepts are, and remain, signed – 'Aristotle's substance, Descartes' cogito, Leibniz's monad, Kant's condition, Shelling's power' – some of them 'make do with an ordinary everyday word that is filled with harmonics so distant that it risks being imperceptible to nonphilosophical ears', while others 'must be indicated by an extraordinary and sometimes even barbarous or shocking word' (Deleuze and Guattari 1994: 7–8). It is precisely because of the invention

Deleuze Studies 8.3 (2014): 314–323
DOI: 10.3366/dls.2014.0151
© Daniela Angelucci
www.euppublishing.com/dls

of new concepts, at times conveyed by ordinary words presented in a new light while at others invoked by means of unexpected neologisms, that Deleuze shows the intertwinement of the two practices, the one artistic and the other conceptual; an intertwinement that does not take place when one reflects on the other, but rather when we realise that both should answer with their own proper tools the very same issue, as 'the tremors are the same, but the fields are different' (Deleuze 2006: 284). The chief feature of cinema is in fact its unexpected approach to exhibiting spiritual life, so that it can be said that it partakes in the history of art and thought.[1]

The preface to *The Movement-Image* presents the work as a taxonomy, a classification of cinematographic signs explicitly referring to the categories as they have been elaborated in Charles S. Peirce's logic. It is however in the following paragraph that we find named the real tutelary deity of the work, that is Henri Bergson, to whom Deleuze had already dedicated a collection of essays twenty years earlier (Deleuze 1991a). Now, in what way does this reiterated encounter between these two philosophers take place? The punctual and even unprejudiced attitude of his remarks on Bergson as developed in the two texts under consideration says something important about Deleuze's idea of the history of philosophy.

We find the finest explanation in François Zourabichvili's *Deleuze: A Philosophy of the Event* (2012), which, by offering a key to understanding Deleuze's distinctive philosophical commentary, individuates its peculiarity in the original usage of the 'free indirect discourse'. The reference here is to Pasolini's notion of *free indirect discourse* in literature and *free indirect subjectivity* in cinema, understood as the possibility to 'speak directly ... in the first person' (Pasolini 2005: 185).[2] It is with this expression stolen from Pasolini, that Zourabichvili described the continuous confrontation of Deleuze with the authors he comments on: rather than a re-elaboration of the thought surveyed, what takes place is an exchange, a process of giving and borrowing. Both in the case of the quotation of thinkers in his texts, and in that of the monographs each dedicated to a specific philosopher (not only Bergson, but also Nietzsche, Kant, Leibniz and Hume) or to a particular artist (Francis Bacon, Marcel Proust), in fact there emerges a common cause between the commentator and the one being commented on which makes their thoughts rather indiscernible. This is exactly what takes place in the two volumes on cinema, which can be also read as an original and privileged pathway to the philosophy of Bergson and, at the very same time, as an approach to the thought of Deleuze having the advantage of immediately exhibiting his philosophical roots.

If, as we shall see, the four theses on cinema – two on movements in the first volume and two others on time in the second one – are presented as commentaries on Bergson's thought, then we can say that, in the first place, Deleuze borrows the very notion of image from *Matter and Memory*. Such a notion defines matter as it is understood by common sense, which is resistant to accepting the idea of both something whose existence is independent from the subject perceiving it, and of an object whose existence depends on its being perceived. Before any philosophising, that is before any sort of realism and idealism, we employ the language of images, as Bergson wrote in the Preface of the seventh edition of his book:

> Matter, in our view, is an aggregate of 'images'. And by 'image' we mean a certain existence which is more than that which the idealist calls a *representation*, but less than that which the realist calls a *thing* – an existence placed halfway between the 'thing' and the 'representation'. (Bergson 1988: 9)

II.

Moving from this substantial affinity, *The Movement-Image* is inspired by Bergson and, paradoxically, by his critique of cinema, which in the last chapter of *Creative Evolution* is depicted precisely as false movement. Bergson writes:

> Such is the contrivance of the cinematograph. And such is also that of our knowledge. Instead of attaching ourselves to the inner becoming of things, we place ourselves outside them in order to recompose their becoming artificially. We take snapshots, as it were, of the passing reality, and, as these are characteristic of the reality, we have only to string them on a becoming, abstract, uniform and invisible, situated at the back of the apparatus of knowledge, in order to imitate what there is that is characteristic in this becoming itself. (Bergson 1944: 332)

Deleuze will return to those pages in order to affirm, contrary to Bergson, how deeply Bergsonian cinematographic art is once presented as that image having movement, understood as unpredictability and creation, as its essence. Cinema is thus not a sum of still sections recon-structed a posteriori with the addition of movement, as mobility belongs already to its smallest unity, the sequence shot, which is a section of the duration scale witnessing a continuous qualitative modification. Deleuze opposes Bergson's thesis with the idea of movement as a constitutive, ontological state, an immediate given of the cinematographic image understood not as an image of the object in movement but rather as *movement-image*. In cinema, the static points of false movement are replaced by shots, intrinsically mobile sections which, by determining the relationship between the elements of the definite whole selected by the framing, qualitatively modify at the same time the whole film.

The idea of cinema as adhesion to reality in its unpredictability, and thus as a device whose specificity is that of rendering movement and duration, can be found even before Deleuze in the reflection of André Bazin, to which I will return when discussing the themes of modernity and chance. If the photographic lens shoulder the burden once carried by the plastic arts by taking advantage of a 'transfer of reality' running from the thing to its reproduction made possible by its automatic genesis, the birth of cinema winds up a process launched by photography, adding to the image of things that of their movement and duration: in this sense what is shown is not a simple reproduction, but rather the 'digital imprint' of reality.

According to Deleuze, movement as qualitative transformation functions in two diverse directions, one relative and one absolute: in respect to what is framed, as the constitution of relationships internal to a closed system, and in respect to the whole – determined by a montage which is already anticipated and envisaged in the shot – as the expression of the duration which does not cease from changing. With this idea of montage as a general compositional principle, Deleuze joins an already well-established tradition, which starting with Eisenstein aimed at portraying it as a procedure of general organisation, that is, as a relationship between the various parts which is not established a posteriori, but which is rather already in place in the sequence shot. The shot, the movement-image, is the mobile section of the duration, the translation of the parts, the transformation of the whole. However, if the framing necessarily determines though its process of constitution an out-of-field (*hors-champ*) – which is not only an extension of the scene, a 'relative elsewhere', but also and most importantly a 'radical Elsewhere', a 'dimension of the spirit' – then the duration of the film is also an opening to the absolute. It is the montage, by operating on the figures already in motion, to extract the idea, the duration; the mobile sections embody in this way the image of time, an indirect image because it is independent and subordinated to movement. Deleuze writes:

> The only generality about montage is that it puts the cinematographic image into a relationship with the whole; that is, with time conceived as the Open.

> In this way it gives an indirect image of time, simultaneously in the individual movement-image and in the whole of the film. On the one hand, it is the variable present; on the other the immensity of future and past. (Deleuze 1986: 55)

Despite the shot being a unity in movement, some interruptions will always emerge in the montage so as to remind us how if on the one side there are the parts and their relative correspondence within a given system, still the Whole is elsewhere. These fractures in the montage do not witness the discontinuity of cinema, but rather remind us of its changing continuity: that is, the absolute one of duration. By breaking the unity into two or three sets, the usage of the false connection in cinema becomes thus a flight from the relative continuity of the closed system, the exhibition of a twist that is already an attitude of the spirit showing the dimension of the Open.

III.

If the first comment to Bergson can be characterised as a confutation of his critique of cinema in the direction of an acknowledgement, in this art, of the full manifestation of the Bergsonian duration, the second comment makes use of the first chapter of *Matter and Memory* – titled 'Of the Selection of Images for Conscious Presentation. What Our Body Means and Does' – with the goal in mind to track down and describe the three mutations of the movement-image: the *perception-image*, in its partial and selective grasping of the object; its extension in the reaction, that is, the *action-image*; and the gap between the two, a hesitating interval on the part of the subject which makes possible the manifestation of pure qualities, free from any kind of utility, distinctive of the *affection-image*. Departing from the assumption of the identity between movement and image Deleuze sketches a classification of the diverse modes of the cinematographic image and of the corresponding indirect marks of time, in a continuous passage from theory to concrete cinematographic examples.

To begin with perception, the speculative premise of Bergson's thought is that of the quasi-coincidence between perception and thing:

> For it is possible to sum up our conclusions as to pure perception by saying that there is in matter something more than, but not something different from, that which is actually given. Undoubtedly, conscious perception does not compass the whole of matter, since it consists, in as far as it is conscious, in the separation, or the 'discernment,' of that which, in matter, interests our

various needs. But between this perception of matter and matter itself there is but a difference of degree and not of kind, pure perception standing toward matter in the relation of the part to the whole. (Bergson 1988: 71)

The perception of objects or of the images of matter would thus be constituted of those very objects, only framed from the point of view of another particular image. The distinction between perceiving and what is perceived is thus for Bergson only a matter of degree: while things are complete, objective images, perception is subtractive and selective, since it is a function of the interests of the subject. The definition of *perception-image*, the first modality of any cinematographic image, moves from these theses, overcoming at the same time the duality of subject and object at work in natural perception in order to delineate a precise statute of cinematographic perception, which consists in a 'being-with' of character and camera:

> It is a case of going beyond the subjective and the objective towards a pure Form which sets itself up as an autonomous vision of content. We are no longer faced with subjective *or* objective images; we are caught in a correlation between a perception-image and a camera-consciousness. (Deleuze 1986: 74)

Here Deleuze is envisioning an entwinement between two diverse perspectives: the empirical subject, the character, who acts, and the transcendental one, the camera-consciousness, watching him or her acting and reflecting on him or her. Here we encounter once more the free indirect subjective: 'the fundamental characteristic of the "free indirect point-of-view shot" is not linguistic but stylistic ... [It can thus] be defined as an interior monologue lacking both the explicit conceptual element and the explicit abstract philosophical element' (Pasolini 2005: 178).

As reaction and unavoidable extension, the perceptual moment of the image corresponds to the active modality – *the action-image* – representing the second pole of the sensory-motor scheme; perception selects the elements, curving the universe so that the action will hit the functional aspect of the percept, which in turn is already directed and predisposed to action itself. The suspension, in the interval created between the perception and the hesitant action, is occupied by the third mutation of the image, the *affection-image*. Here the movements, which do not remain images of perception nor become action, are absorbed by the subject as expressions and pure quality. The appearance of affectivity in the image is made available by what might be labelled as 'retracted action', to borrow Maurizio Grande's expression (in particular, in reference to expressionist cinema):

> The zone of indeterminacy of a living being allows one not to act nor to react, that is to substitute action with the expression of affectivity, of the subject's interiority conveyed by one's face – which, in its turn, becomes the glaring reflection of the affects, potentialities, and qualitative transformations of affects through a retracted action, an action we might label as *internal to the affections*. (Grande 2003: 386; original emphasis; my translation)

These movements of subjectivity characterise each film, and yet, despite there being no single work made up of a single kind of image, still one of the three species is always dominant in a certain author or genre of film, as it will be evident in the framing, in the shot or in the montage.

The archetypical work of affection-image, featuring the expressive presence of close-ups and the representation of an indefinite, anonymous space, is *The Passion of Joan of Arc* (1926) by Dreyer, 'an almost exclusively affective film'. The very exhibition of affective and sensible qualities is noticeable in Bresson's characters, in Rohmer's stories, in Bergman's close-ups and in Antonioni's colours. The typical cinematographic genres of action-image, characterised by both realism and a well-determined space and time, are instead the documentary (one might think of Flaherty's *Nanook* (1922), in which the actions of the leading character modify the environment by attenuating its hostility), the psycho-social film (Deleuze's example is the realistic look of King Vidor's production as displayed in *The Crowd*) (1928), as well as the detective story and western, in which the transformation of the initial situation through the characters' conduct follows a narrative thread which usually leads to the re-establishment of order.[3]

Besides the three fundamental modalities Deleuze individuates other models as well: the *impulse-image* – a 'degenerate affect' or 'embryonic action' determined between the idealism of affection and the realism of the act, characteristic of Buñuel's films such as *The Exterminating Angel* (1962) or *Simon of the Desert* (1965) – the *reflection-image*, intermediary between action and the *relation-image*, the last variation of the cinema of movement which goes beyond the sensory-motor scheme and guides the passage to the time-image. By overcoming – to use Peirce's terminology – the self-referring firstness of the affect as well as the secondness of the act (a dual moment in itself as it gets realised in the perception act, thus referring to itself only through something other), the relation-image constitutes itself as thirdness, introducing a third term connecting the other objects in place. According to Deleuze, the introduction of the mental image as thirdness, that is, a relationship between the objects and the other images, takes place with Hitchcock's cinema, whose crime plot often introduces the figure of the witness as third – as in the case of the paralysed James Stewart forced to observe in *Rear Window* (1954). Deleuze writes:

> There is not only the acting and the action, the assassin and the victim, there is always a third and not accidental or apparent third, as a suspected innocent would be, but a fundamental third constituted by the relation itself, the relation of the assassin, of the victim or of the action with the apparent third ... This perpetual tripling also takes over objects, perceptions, affections. (Deleuze 1986: 201)

As Deleuze explains at the beginning of the volume on time while summarising the images and signs of classical cinema, there does not exist an intermediate moment between perception-image and affection because perception functions here as an ideal zero grade, that is, as a necessary moment which is presupposed by the other modalities, which necessarily constitute themselves as its continuation. With thirdness there appears in films a reflexive, relative element that jeopardises the duality of action, in this way letting other kinds of sign emerge.

The summary of the proper forms of the cinematographic system of action and of movement taking place at the beginning of the second volume allows Deleuze to measure up with the two principles of Metz's semiology: the idea that cinema is constitutively narrative and that the shot is the smallest narrative utterance. His answer moves once again from the fundamental presupposition of movement as the most authentic and immediate given of the cinematographic image: the narration would not be one among its given elements, but rather determined as a consequence derived from the combination (montage) of images themselves. These, on the other hand, cannot be substituted by utterances because in this way they would be deprived of the essential dimension of movement. In this sense it can be said that the image is an utterable more than an utterance, that is, a sign of reality which might virtually become discourse and narration. The advantage of Peirce's semiotics, whose classification is surveyed in greater detail in the second volume, is that, at least in the beginning of the semiosis, signs are not conceived from the point of view of language, but rather from the point of view of the phenomenon itself.

IV.

The decline of the action-image is thus a constitutive aspiration of cinema, which ever since its beginnings took the form of a vocation – shared with literature – to go beyond the unitary dramatic plot: it is a representative structure carrying within itself the very possibilities and ambition of its own overcoming. That cinema has as its intimate essence the conditions of its modification, and that its actuality is produced by its progression leaving open the possibility and the necessity of the encounter with the unforeseeable, shows evidence of its Bergsonism. *The movement-image*, begun with the critique of Bergson's statement on cinema, ends up acknowledging the cinematographic image with the very essence of movement and duration:

> There is always a moment when the cinema meets the unforeseeable or the improvisation, the irreducibility of a present living under the present of narration, and the camera cannot even begin its work without engendering its own improvisations, both as obstacles and as indispensable means. There two themes, the open totality and the event in the course of happening, are part of the profound Bergsonianism of the cinema in general. (Deleuze 1986: 206)

The movement-image, having reached its limits, extends from relation-image to the mental-image, questioning its very statute with the appearance of a third element which breaks the duality of the sensory-motor scheme, and initiating a crisis in the action system representing the classical form of representational cinema. The final break of these schemes takes place only when the relation-image is not considered as the realisation of the traditional system any more, as it happened in the United States at the time of its birth, but rather as the conscious passage to a new order. The social, economic, political and ethical reasons of such a crisis were fully in place in post-war Italy, in the next decade in France and in the following one in Germany, as long as the essence of modern cinema got expressed in the urgency to abandon realism and the narrative form so as to unleash what Deleuze defines as *opsigns* and *sonsigns*, that is, purely optical and sound situations unrelated to any perceptive reference and dislocated in a void space.

In this way movement gets rid of its logical schemes, the intertwinements between perception and act, and loses its centre of determination, through which it was able to control time by indirectly representing it through the montage of the essentially mobile sections. The revelation of an aberrant and a-centred movement discloses another image that allows time – already in place before any happening – to emerge immediately. The dispersive situations typical of modern cinema, albeit free from any relationship of cause–effect and characterised by discontinuity and fragmentation, create in fact yet another kind of bond; that is, they relate directly with thought and time making them 'sensible' and 'visible and audible'. The third and fourth commentaries on Bergson elaborated in *The Time-Image* analyse the deep meaning of this sketch of time as well as of its two dimensions of past and present in modern films:

> If normal movement subordinates the time of which it gives us an indirect representation, aberrant movement speaks up for an anteriority of time that it presents to us directly, on the basis of the disproportion of scales, the dissipation of centers and the false continuity of the images themselves. (Deleuze 1989: 37)

Notes

1. For the relationship between philosophy and cinema, see Angelucci 2013.
2. According to Pasolini, the closeness and the exchanges between the style of the author and the mood of the character depicted represent the conditions of possibility of a cinema of poetry; a cinema that would embody the nature of the cinematographic images as a 'natural language of reality'.
3. Deleuze further divides the action-image into Large and Small form: while the former follows an S A S' scheme, according to which an initial situation is outstripped by a different one through some kind of action, the latter is characterised by an A S A' scheme for which the initial action reveals a situation which invites a new action.

Time

I.

Proceeding from the coincidence between image and movement, the two comments to Bergson elaborated in *The Time-Image* investigate the characteristics of the new cinema of opsigns and sonsigns, situations which do not respond to – and are thus unrestricted by – the sensory-motor scheme. In this kind of film, movement naturally continues to be part of the image as its constitutive datum, and yet what steps in the foreground is time – temporality 'in person', as Deleuze writes – and its mechanisms. The direct performance of time in image, the essential novelty of modern cinema, allows Deleuze to get Bergson slightly closer to Kantian philosophy: by defining time as a pure form of subjectivity, Bergson operated the first reversal of the relationship between time and movement in the direction of the subordination of the latter to the former.

A synthesis of Kantian philosophy in relationship to this reversal of the concept of temporality appears in the 1986 Deleuzian essay 'On Four Poetic Formulas Which Might Summarize the Kantian Philosophy'. The liberation of pure, non-chronological time completed by Kant is here resumed by Deleuze in the poetic formula 'the time is out of joint' – a line pronounced by Hamlet, the tragic hero par excellence who brings to bear the emancipation of time:

> Time is out of joint, the door off its hinges, signifies the first great Kantian reversal: movement is now subordinated to time. Time is no longer related to the movement it measures, but rather to the time that conditions it. Moreover, movement is no longer the determination of objects, but the description of a space, a space we must set aside in order to discover time as the condition of action. (Deleuze 1998: 27–8)

In his third comment on Bergson, the first in the volume on time, Deleuze reprises the theses presented in the second chapter of *Matter*

Deleuze Studies 8.3 (2014): 324–333
DOI: 10.3366/dls.2014.0152
© Daniela Angelucci
www.euppublishing.com/dls

and Memory dedicated to 'Of the Recognition of Images', distinguishing two different kinds of perceptual response: a habitual, mechanical one, configured as a sort of mechanical reaction of sensory-motor extension of perception itself, consisting in an '*instantaneous* recognition, of which the body is capable by itself' (Bergson 1988: 92); and an attentive, active one, characterised instead by the appearance of a hesitation when facing the perceived reality, an uncertainty in the response forcing the subject to reflect and search in his or her memory, similar to the way the camera gets a certain figure into focus. In the former type of recognition the reaction movement takes place on the very same level of the perceived object, while in the latter the subject examines his or her past before coming back to the present moving through several different dimensions in always novel circular – more or less wide – movements, which Bergson, by offering a geometrical scheme (Bergson 1988: 104), called circuits, 'circles of memory'. If the result of habitual perception is the sensory-motor image – the thing itself, exhibited in classical, narrative cinema films – in the case of attentive recognition, what is attained is a pure optical and sound image, a description of the object.

The affective-image as well, first presented in the volume dedicated to movement, is defined as what inhabits the interval between perception and reaction (as we shall see, Deleuze's critique of Jacques Rancière will revolve around this proximity). However, in Deleuze's description, affection widens the perceptual matter on its very sensory-motor dimension, while the pure optical and sound image produces a different element which does not extend but rather fulfils the gap: the dimension of the spirit or temporality, enabling the activity of the subject to attain a whole new sense. The pure optical image, which at first appears as poorer in content and more rarefied as it substitutes the thing rather than presenting it, will reveal itself as richer and more 'typical' than the former, in which perception is distracted by the activity of selection of the sensory-motor scheme in view of the action:

> Conversely, the pure optical image may be only a description, and concern a character who no longer knows how or is no longer able to react to the situation; the restraint of this image, the thinness of what it retains, line or simple point, 'slight fragment without importance', bring the thing each time to an essential singularity, and describe the inexhaustible, endlessly referring to other descriptions. (Deleuze 1989: 45)

If the sensory-motor image originates from the linear nexus between perception and reaction accompanying the narrative procedure in cinema, the answer to the question about the identity of levels, the circuits enacted by the activity of attention in perception, and thus by the pure optical image, is much more problematical to obtain. According to Bergson, the answer consists in recollection-images, recalled in the memory by the subject during the perceptual hesitation. Deleuze opens up the range of possibilities by suggesting a series of couples in which it is essential to bear in mind that the two terms are *by nature* different: the real and the imaginary, the physical and the mental, the actual and the virtual. The linear links making possible the extension of objective perception in the associated reaction get progressively more complex, become circular and, in the continuous passage between the two different ontological dimensions, represent 'the layers of one and the same physical reality, and the levels of one and the same mental reality, memory or spirit' (Deleuze 1989: 46). It is a perpetual oscillation between two indiscernible and yet distinct moments, in which to each aspect of the perceived thing there corresponds a recollection, a thought connected via a circuit which simultaneously creates and delete its image, a unity constituted by the coalescence of all its visited and contradicted sheets. The Deleuzian definition runs as follows: 'The purely optical and sound situation (description) is an actual image, but one which, instead of extending into movement, links up with a virtual image and forms a circuit with it' (Deleuze 1989: 47).

But what, in cinema, plays the role of the virtual? I want to go straight to the answer offered by Deleuze, leaving aside for the moment the path covered to achieve it – a path which I shall survey in detail in the next chapter dedicated to this concept. The immediate and always reversible virtual double of the actual gets actualised as a point of 'indiscernibility' between the two ontologically different dimensions; such a virtual double is what Deleuze calls the *crystal-image*, that is, the heart and root of pure optical and sound images:

> But here we see that the opsign finds its true generic element when the actual optical image crystallizes with *its own* virtual image, on the small internal circuit. This is a crystal-image, which gives us the key, or rather the 'heart', of opsigns and their composition. The latter are nothing other than slivers of crystal-images. (Deleuze 1989: 69)

II.

In crystals – an ordinary word granted a new meaning, like the practice of inventing concepts acquires a new meaning – 'there is this mutual search – blind and halting – of matter and spirit' (Deleuze 1989: 75). The actual and the virtual engage in a continuous exchange, so that the two moments, although distinct, are not discernible, as they find their existence and meaning only in their reciprocal presupposition, in their being one relative to the other: a virtuality is constituted as such only in relationship and opposition to an actuality of which it constitutes the virtual, and vice versa. This indiscernible bond is not the result of a subjective, psychological impression (in that case it would in fact only consist in an inability to distinguish them, the fruit of confusion or error), but is rather an 'objective illusion' of the image, as its duplicity is constitutive to its very nature.

The aesthetic figures proper of the structure of crystal are a series of pairs representing ways in which the couple of actual–virtual can be articulated: the opaque–limpid couple – which already gets manifested in the interplay between the visible and the obscure character of acting a certain role, in which the actor hides him- or herself and leaves the character to emerge – and the seed-surrounding couple – which instead expresses the circulation of potentialities as a germination and transformation of the surroundings. Whether the determinations of classical cinema – that is perception, action and affection – often find their cinematographic equivalent in a general characterisation of film, Deleuze individuates various poetic concretisations of the crystal-image in the objects, details and recurring motifs of many films of modern cinema: the mirror[1] reflecting the virtual figure of an actual character – think about, among the many mentioned films, some selected scenes of Losey's *The Servant* (1963), the end of Orson Welles' *The Lady from Shanghai* (1947) or the hotel of Alain Resnais's *Last Year at Marienbad*; (1961) the ship, with the upper part above the waterline visible and limpid, and the lower part hidden below the waterline and opaque (as, for example, in Federico Fellini's *And the Ship Sails On*, 1983); and the rain, which reveals itself as the seed of change in some movies by Akira Kurosawa (for example, already in *Rashomon*, 1950) and Michelangelo Antonioni (for example, *The Night*, dated 1961, in which the rain represents the sign of a transformation in the life of the characters).

However, besides the configurations of the crystal-image, what interests Deleuze is its genesis: the crystal is 'the most fundamental operation of time', constantly splitting into a past tending to its self-preservation and a passing present leaning towards the future. This differentiation into two dimensions – which, however, coexist and do not cease to swap and convert into each other, despite always in the process of their differentiation – represents accurately the Bergsonian definition of non-chronological time, and shows also 'what we see' exhibited in the image of the crystal as its genetic element and constitutive structure: 'what we see in the crystal is time itself, a bit of time in the pure state' (Bergson 1989: 82).

> The crystal reveals a direct time-image, and no longer an indirect image of time deriving from movement. It does not abstract time; it does better: it reverses its subordination in relation to movement. The crystal is like a *ratio cognoscendi* of time, while time, conversely, is *ratio essendi*. What the crystal reveals or makes visible is the hidden ground of time, that is, its differentiation into two flows, that of presents which pass and that of pasts which are preserved. (Bergson 1989: 98)

In modern cinema the crystal appears in different shapes: the typical perfection of Max Ophüls's films (*The Earrings of Madame de . . . , dated 1953*), which conveys the coalescence of actual and virtual in a unitary scene without gaps; the rift typical of the work of Jean Renoir through which, besides the short-circuit of real and imaginary and present and past, a new reality is revealed by means of the substitution of the simple shot with the depth of field, an opening to the future (think of the use of water in Renoir's films, as for example in *Boudu*); the formation and growth resulting from the richness and continuous multiplication of Fellini's images, true revelations of life expanding in its spontaneity; the decomposition, the object of Visconti's cinematography, revealing the historical and natural collapse of a world – not only of a certain social class, but also of a 'spiritual family' – obscured and in decline.

III.

The occasion of a perspicuous understanding of the radical difference and of the continuous exchange between present and past, actual and virtual, as well as of the preservation of pure recollections, is offered by the Bergsonian scheme of the inverse cone at play in the third chapter of *Matter and Memory*. The apex of the cone, occupied by the representation of the constantly progressing present, rests on the plane of actuality, while the volume represents the totality of recollections, the memory in itself, by nature different from the dimension of experience and yet always in potential contact with it: if pure recollection gets revealed to the sensory-motor mechanisms in its totality – thus allowing the body to react and accomplish the task suggested by the present – such mechanisms would facilitate the unconscious and idle recollections descending from the heights of pure memory to materialise and come back to life, focusing on action. According to Deleuze, this scheme is particularly apt to represent the first non-chronological image of time, the one grounded in the past which gets preserved: in fact, the volume of the cone efficaciously depicts a memory which is *déjà-là*, which pre-exists and in which we move in the search for recollections; not some mental and interior state, but a Being-memory, a world-memory, a pure virtuality that we penetrate and in which we lose ourselves. In the geometrical figure the coexistence of the diverse moments of the past also appears evident, the more or less wide sections of the cone, each of which contains at the same time the totality of recollections:

> Between the past as pre-existence in general and the present as infinitely contracted past there are, therefore, all the circles of that past constituting so many stretched or shrunk *regions*, *strata*, and *sheets*: each region with its own characteristics, its 'tones', its 'aspects', its 'singularities', its 'shining points', and its 'dominant' figures. (Deleuze 1989: 99)

We settle – or 'jump' as Deleuze writes – in one of the two circles of memory depending on the different quality of the recollection sought through the diverse sheets of our past.

In the picture of the cone the statute of the present is also immediately apparent as a narrower and more contracted point than the past, as its extreme limit; a present which elapses in the very moment in which it is perceived, 'its pure present being the invisible progress of the past gnawing into the future' (Bergson 1988: 150). If, however, the present in itself is considered as stripped of its actuality – as the pure recollection was freed from the necessity of its actualisation in a recollection-image – we obtain the second direct figure of time, grounded on the contracted present of the apex of the cone, the 'peaks of present' freed from their sensory-motor extension. The present becomes thus an ecstatic dimension removed from its function of converting recollections into acts, a function of which Deleuze, making reference to Augustine's thought, exhibits in three simultaneous elements: *memory* (present of the past), *attention* (present of the present) and *wait* (present of the future).

> We find ourselves here in a direct time-image of a different kind from the previous one: no longer the coexistence of sheets of past, but the simultaneity of peaks of present. We therefore have two kinds of chronosigns: the first are *aspects* (regions, layers), the second *accents* (peaks of view [*pointes de vue*]). (Bergson 1989: 101)

The figure of time in person depicting the past in general despite its sheets appears in what Deleuze considers as the first film of modern cinema: namely, *Citizen Kane* (1941) by Orson Welles, the first director who showed a time-image exploring entire sections of the past in their existence. In the film the writer of a newsreel is given the task of reconstructing the life of the tycoon Charles Foster Kane following his death: after reading his diaries, the journalist interviews his second wife, the head of the board of governors of his newspaper, his best friend and the butler who assisted him during his last years. The goal of the inquiry is that of discovering the meaning of the mysterious word uttered by Kane on his deathbed, but the enigma is revealed only to the eyes of the spectators – and not to those of the characters – in the last scene, in which is filmed a pile of by then useless objects once belonging to the protagonist in the past being thrown into the fire by the attendants: 'Rosebud' is the sign impressed on the wooden sled with which Kane used to play during his childhood.[2]

Each witness who gets interrogated about the life of the protagonist represents a section, a virtual sheet of his past, which, however, is unable to designate a re-enacted recollection, that is, a 'presentified' image which has lost its past character, as it was happening in the flashbacks typical of movement. Moving from Bergson's distinction between *recollection-image*, which actualises the past in relationship to the present in function of what it perceives, and the *pure recollection*, which should keep the mark of virtuality, Deleuze translates cinematographically this distinction by individuating a difference between flashbacks, that is, the 'presentifying' past, and sheets of the past, that is, exhibition of pure recollection in itself. Here the story, that is, the point of view of each witness on the various parts of the life of the protagonist, leads to the evocation of entire regions of virtuality precisely because it is unable to find what it was looking for and actualise it in a recollection-image. The evocation takes place not through the transformation of the past into actuality, but rather by jumping into another ontological dimension, that is, by settling itself from the present into pure recollection.

All the stylistic innovations produced by Welles with the collaboration of the director of photography Gregg Toland aim precisely at the liberation of time in itself: the use of *deep focus* with the goal of keeping contemporaneously in focus all the elements and scales of the shot; the use of the grand wide-angle lens, which enormously widens close-ups and pushes the background away; the particular illumination, emphasising volumes provoking a stark contrast between light and shadow; the shots from bottom up or from unusual angles. The result is a depth of field that substitutes a simple juxtaposition of plans and levels independent from each other with the construction of a diagonal perspective, in which the background is in communication with the foreground as well as with the intermediate levels. Welles' aim is not only that of forcing the spectator 'to "read" all the sheets of the image, as the actions eventually taking place in the background are not inert and merely decorative anymore but rather true active operators of dramaturgy' (Provenzano 1994: 125; my translation). The liberation of this profundity allows in the first place the appearance of the *continuum* of Bergsonian duration, of the temporal dimension that, once emancipated from the subordination of space, shows itself freely. In its function of remembering, the novel conception of the depth of field allows Welles to represents also its misfortunes, the temporal disorders illuminating its double structure, its virtual side:

> The sheets of past exist, they are strata from where we draw our recollection-images. But either they are in any case unusable, because death is a permanent present, the most contracted region; or they can no longer be recalled because they are breaking up and becoming twisted, scattered in a non-stratified region. (Deleuze 1989: 115)

In *Citizen Kane* we see realised the two cases of 'illness of memory' about which Bergson wrote. The first one, in which the recollection cannot be invoked any more, represents the running theme of the film: Rosebud is an element of the life of Kane so distant and buried in the past that the images pass by and touch slightly without being able to catch and centre it, and the recollections of those who were closer to him in life are completely ineffective. The second case, in which the recollection is still evocable but cannot be utilised any more, can be appreciated in the film as well: all the images of the life of the protagonist recalled by the witnesses are revealed as useless, as there is no present able to accommodate them because of Kane's death, which imposes itself in the first scene as an unavoidable premise. At the end of the film the meaning of the word 'Rosebud' is revealed in vain, being literally 'for no one'.

In this as well as in other Welles films, the parabola of recollections – which are unable to emerge from the past or rather reappear only to fade into the void[3] – is according to Deleuze not representative of a sort of nihilism the way he understands it, whose profound sense would simply lie in the vanity of human existence. The significance of the unavoidability or the idleness of the past symbolises the origin of the 'permanent state of crisis' of the concept of time, which, by emancipating itself from the subordination of movement, forces its joints to reveal hallucinatory presences, the coexistence of diverse moments, and paradoxical connections. In *Citizen Kane* 'all the coexistent strata are in touch and adjacent to each other' (Deleuze 1989: 115), and time secures its autonomy also through the reports of the witnesses, who are unable to solve the mystery, but who in their reports evoke events which they cannot objectively know. It is the disease of the memory, the impossibility of remembering or making use of the recollection, the incapacity to discern the various moments of the past jeopardising the very idea of truth.

The image of time as the contraction and de-actualised peaks of the present makes instead its appearance in many films of the late Buñuel. If in *The Movement-Image* Deleuze mentioned the director as a representative of affection cinema, a type of cinema in which the power of impulses emerges with emphasis, its late works, by abandoning the naturalistic perspective and the scheme of perception–action, seem to attain a vision of the image as the manifestation of different and simultaneous worlds. In this way, the finale of *Belle de jour* (1967) shows in the protagonist's husband a paralysis that took place and yet did not take place; also, *The Discreet Charm of the Bourgeoisie* (1972) offers different and irreducible versions of the very same lunch, not subjective and imaginary points of view, but rather 'different objective worlds' disclosing simultaneously.

Both figures of non-chronological time are present in the film by Alain Resnais, written and directed with the collaboration of Alain Robbe-Grillet, *Last Year at Marienbad*, which fully conveys the crisis of imagination-action and the emergence of the elements of modernity: the nomadic characters, the accumulation of cliché, the appearance of thought as the only true protagonist. The story is that of a confrontation between the irreducibly different memories of a man and a woman confronting and evoking two diverse and incommensurable pasts; it is in fact only the man who can remember what happened during the last year in Marienbad and wants to persuade the woman about his recollection. Deleuze attributes to Resnais the interest for the past and its virtual sheets, as well as for its jeopardisation dictated by abandonment of a fixed centre from which to observe it (which in the films by Welles could have been individuated, for example, in the death of Kane, while here it disappears for a multi-voiced memory, each of which is extraneous and incommensurable to the others); the feminine character, which lives in the passage between two presents, at times suspicious while at others convinced of the version offered to her, is instead more akin to the conception of Robbe-Grillet, oriented towards a perpetual present perpetually divided from its actuality. It might well be that the two characters of the film settle on two different regions of memory, preventing them from having the same recollections, but it might also be that the authors meant to create what Deleuze defines as a 'sheet *of* transformation' – paradoxical, hypnotic, hallucinogenic – allowing the communication between fragments belonging to different ages, which establishes a continuity between the elements of the different levels.

The 'crystalline' cinema, which has abandoned the regime of action and causal connections in favour of an image which 'no longer has space and movement as its primary characteristics but topology and time' (Deleuze 1989: 125), aspires to the creation of a virtual sheet pervading all the others, it 'rolls them up and unrolls them', radically questioning identity as a principle of representation and arriving at a narration which goes beyond truth and falsity, beyond the actual and the virtual.

Notes

1. In this sense, meta-cinema, that is, the many reflections on cinema conducted through the cinematographic medium, would not be, according to Deleuze, a testimony of a lack of vitality, of the plunging of the cinematographic art to its 'death', but rather one of the modalities typical of its enrichment.
2. According to Roberto Campari, the theme of bygone childhood lies at the centre of *Citizen Kane*, as he argues in his *Film della memoria. Mondi perduti, ricordati e sognati* (2005); in an interpretation already in place in the volume by André Bazin, *Orson Welles* (1992) – which still represents an authoritative reference in the vast literature on the director – which does not stand in contradiction with the one offered by Deleuze, in which, however, the loss of the past is devoid of any individual and psychological connotation.
3. In *Mr. Arkadin* (1955), for example, the past gets re-evoked only to be cancelled and destroyed as well: the private investigator recruited by Arkadin to investigate his own past explores the virtual sheets, but such an exploration aims at eliminating all that comes to light. In his work on this film, Michele Bertolini did not neglect the link between fiction and time's disharmony (see Bertolini 2004).

Virtual

I.

In order to trace the path that brings Deleuze to the individuation of the crystal-image as the nucleus of the exchange between actual and virtual, an exchange enabling modern cinema to represent the genesis of time, we should go back to Bergson, and more precisely to the two kinds of perceptual response sketched in *Matter and Memory*. As already noted, for Bergson there is a habitual, automatic recognition having roughly the form of a mechanical reaction to perception itself, and an attentive recognition, characterised instead by a kind of hesitation, an uncertainty inducing the subject to reflect and inquire into his or her memory.

If the sensory-motor image originates from the linear link connecting perception and reaction that constitutes the relations of cause–effect structuring the narrative procedures, the question raised during attentive recognition lying at the base of the pure optical image will be much more complex to address. Linear links become circular and enact a continuous exchange between two ontologically different dimensions, that is, past and present, two indiscernible and yet distinct moments united by a bond according to which each aspect of the perceived thing corresponds to a recollection, to a thought. The two dimensions through which this perpetual exchange takes place, that is, the actual and the virtual, the present and the past, would thus necessarily coexist – a quite shocking and unsettling statement, which will be thematised in a progressively assertive way, but which in the pages dedicated to the pure optical image initially appears almost as a platitude. In this context it would thus be worth repeating the already quoted definition of this image of modern cinema offered by Deleuze: 'The purely optical and sound situation (description) is an actual image, but one which, instead of extending

Deleuze Studies 8.3 (2014): 334–341
DOI: 10.3366/dls.2014.0153
www.euppublishing.com/dls

into movement, links up with a virtual image and forms a circuit with it' (Deleuze 1989: 47).

It is also worth repeating at this stage the question on the nature and genesis of the virtual, this time following the details of the path covered by the author for its full articulation. As a first step Deleuze takes Bergson's suggestion by analysing recollection-images and their connection with the actual in cinema via the flashback. This procedure, announced by fading effects or conveyed by the overlapping of images, constitutes a conventional and extrinsic method which allows the linear progression of the narration or alternatively displays the deviation and bifurcation of time, showing enigmatically, for example, all the possible effects of a certain situation. The precise moment in which the situation splits, in which the possibility of a deviation gets revealed – a moment which cannot but display itself afterwards – is, for instance, often at the centre of some scenes of the films by Joseph Manckiewicz; for example, in a flashback scene of *All About Eve* the recounted character becomes in its turn a narrator, having sensed the duplicity of the woman and what could have had happened. In any case, the flashback falls short of its role, since, besides receiving the justification of its existence from the outside, reveals itself as non-virtual. In fact, it 'does not deliver the past to us, but only represents the former present that the past "was" ', showing in the film a recollection-image already far from pure-recollection, already 'actualized or in process of being made actual, which does not form with the actual, present image a circuit of indiscernibility' (Deleuze 1989: 54).

The Deleuzian conclusion is that actuality enters authentically in contact with virtuality only when perception, unable to form either sensory-motor images or recollection-images, fails in the recognition, thus accommodating sensations without any objective correspondence and which do not extend to the sensory-motor level. The virtual correlate of the pure optical image gets displayed in those disturbances of memory, or 'failures of recognition' – in the hallucinations and in the delirium characteristic of the most extreme situations, but also in everyday dreams and amnesias – which the Soviet expressionist and surrealist cinema elected among the most significant themes of their cinematographic production. This leads us to our second step.

Deleuze refers once again to the second and third chapters of *Matter and Memory*, in which the analysis of the dreaming state is used as confirmation of the conception of the phenomena of memory and recognition just expressed. According to Bergson, the dream is the extreme state of 'an entirely contemplative memory' (Bergson 1988: 155), the possibility of the emergence of the totality of fluctuating recollections given the relaxation of the nervous tension and the collapse of the attention purely directed to action. The dormant person does not cease to receive sensations, but his or her perception does not result in a sensory-motor response either, rather it enters into contact with a mutable and diffused set of recollections and with the past in general. Perception is not connected here with any particular recollection-image, but rather establishes an extremely dispersive and loose connection between actuality and virtuality which Deleuze, reprising the Bergsonian scheme, defines as *'the largest circuit or "the outermost envelope" of all the circuits'* (Deleuze 1989: 56).

In comparison with recollection-image, which gets actualised by responding to the call of the perception-image, the diffused sensations of the dormant person, despite him or her being unconscious about them, provoke the transformation of the virtual into an actual which in its turn becomes the virtuality of the subsequent actualisation, in a process of infinite feedback and chasing: the most vivid cinematographic example is without doubt *An Andalusian Dog* (1928) by Luis Buñuel, with its succession of images in perpetual becoming. The images of the dream, scattered, dissociated and yet ascribable to one single sensation, the initial one which remains implicit and present, are rendered cinematographically in two different modalities: on the one side through fades, complex movements of the camera, special effects; while on the other through simple cuts in the montage, creating an unreal processuality of still real objects. On the one side, rich and overloaded means, while, on the other, ellipses. The law to which they respond is the same: namely, a wide circuit with loose perceptual links in which the preceding makes reference to the succeeding without any interruption.

However, as occurs in the recollection-image actualised in a flashback, in the film the loss of the sensory-motor connection taking place while asleep is compensated most of the time by the use of an explicit dream-image, in which, once again, the indiscernibility of the virtual and the actual is not guaranteed: we have an unaware dreamer and a spectator aware that what he or she observes is not the reality of wakefulness. In order to define these states of estrangement in which this split does not get explicitly manifested, Deleuze uses the notion of 'implied dream', a dream in which the pure optical and sound image – which has lost any automatic extension as well as a seemingly virtual recollection-image or an explicit dream image to which it relates – extends instead in a 'movement of the world', in a depersonalised movement which does not belongs to the character any more, but rather to the space around him or her:

The world takes responsibility for the movement that the subject can no longer or cannot take. This is a virtual movement, but it becomes actual at the price of an expansion of the totality of space and of a stretching of time. It is therefore the limit of the largest circuit. (Deleuze 1989: 59)

The depersonalised movement par excellence is the musical comedy, in which the dancer-actor abandons his or her subjectivity and lets the over-personal movement carry him or her, entering the dance in the 'implied dream'. The dances of Fred Astaire and Gene Kelly give access to another world, but so also do some moments of Vincente Minnelli's films, in which the real and the imaginary become indiscernible. The very same movement of the world characterises the outcomes of the evolution of the burlesque genre, which, starting with the emphasis on sensory-motor situations (Laurel and Hardy), introduces at first some affective elements (Buster Keaton), then mental images (in Groucho Marx's nonsenses), up to provoking a rupture of the sensory-motor bounds in which the character does not act, but rather blends into the movements of the world, in an energy unconsciously sucking, involving and dragging him or her (Jerry Lewis).

Departing from a virtuality correspondent and coalescent to its own actuality, to the co-present reflection of a reality, via the hypothesis of recollection-images we thus reached the great circuit of the explicit or implicit dream-images, the continued succession of indistinguishable moments, representing the widest and most dilated level of the Bergsonian scheme. Isn't this exactly what we were looking for?

Should not the opposite direction have been pursued? Contracting the image instead of dilating it. Searching for the smallest circuit that functions as internal limit for all the others and that puts the actual image besides a kind of immediate, symmetrical, consecutive or even simultaneous double. The broad circuits of recollection in dream assume this narrow base, this extreme point, and not the other way around. (Deleuze 1989: 68)

We thus reached our intended destination: the most contracted circuit, immediate and always reversible virtual reflection of the actual, point of indiscernibility between the two ontologically different dimensions, the root of pure optical and sound images. Here Deleuze truly brings to its extreme consequences the Bergsonian intuition about the relationship between matter and memory in hesitant recognition, and in the following words by Bergson the character of the crystal description can already be appreciated; words which also at the same time show Bergson's greater attention to external reality, although depicted in the immediacy of its opening to the spiritual dimension:

> Every *attentive* perception truly involves a *reflection*, in the etymological sense of the word that is to say the projection, outside ourselves, of an actively created image, identical with, or similar to, the object on which it comes to mold itself. (Bergson 1988: 102)

In the genesis and structure of the crystal-image we see reinstated the radical affirmation of the existence of virtuality in itself, which allows Deleuze to subtract time to its exteriorisation and at the same time rebut the interpretation of Bergsonian duration in terms of internal life and psychological state. If time continuously splits up into present and past, and each moment of life has contemporaneously in itself the two elements of perception and recollection which the crystal embodies in its constitutive double nature, then virtuality – that is, pure recollection, the past, memory, the spirit – exists *outside* one's subjectivity and consciousness, *in* time. It is rather consciousness that, by recalling, gets installed in the virtual, it moves in time, which is thus not internal to the subject but rather gets configured as a 'form of interiority' which the subject *inhabits* and is unable to escape. In this sense the idea of the crystal, as an inorganic mineral, stresses efficaciously the a-subjectivity and over-personal character of Deleuzian time, the radical questioning of personal identity and the refutation of a temporality in terms of the psychological and interior life of the mind. In *Difference and Repetition* (first published in 1968) we already find Deleuze describing virtuality in these terms:

> We opposed the virtual and the real: although it could not have been more precise before now, this terminology must be corrected. The virtual is opposed not to the real but to the actual. *The virtual is fully real in so far as it is virtual.* Exactly what Proust said of states of resonance must be said of the virtual: 'Real without being actual, ideal without being abstract'; and symbolic without being fictional. Indeed, the virtual must be defined as strictly a part of the real object – as though the object had one part of itself in the virtual into which it plunged as though into an objective dimension. (Deleuze 1994: 208–9)

II.

The idea of a duration existing outside one's subjective consciousness, although in constant touch with it, emerges as the central theme of the chapter of *Matter and Memory* titled 'Of the Survival of Images', to which Deleuze refers in his fourth comment on Bergson, following the splitting of the crystal towards the two directions of the past and the present. In those pages Bergson remarked in the first place on the radical difference between the two dimensions: the present, being sensory-motor, consists in sensations and movements, while the past, as pure-recollection, is characterised as un-extensive and divided by perceptions, so that the contact between the two via the recollection-image, that is, the actualisation of a part of the past in view of the action, is not characterised as a gradual passage but rather as a leap between two ontologically distinct moments. This distinction in kind between matter and memory – which, although maintaining its necessity, becomes indiscernible in the smallest circuit (or, if you will, in the Deleuzian crystal) – represents the necessary condition for the existence of a virtual in itself, of a past which, even when idle, gets preserved in its state of latency. Given the definition of the present as *'what is being made'*, what is no longer present would not be what is no more, but rather what is useless, unused, but not for this reason inexistent: thus 'there will no longer be any more reason to say that the past effaces itself as soon as perceived than there is to suppose that material objects cease to exist when we cease to perceive them' (Bergson 1988: 142).[1] Bergson concludes:

> This survival of the past per se forces itself upon philosophers, then, under one form or another; the difficulty that we have in conceiving it comes simply from the fact that we extend to the series of memories, in time, that obligation of containing and being contained which applies only to the collection of bodies instantaneously perceived in space. (Bergson 1988: 149)

The importance in Bergsonian philosophy of the preservation of the past in itself, which according to Deleuze is one of the less understood aspects of Bergsonism, has been already tackled in the essay 'Memory as Virtual Coexistence' (Deleuze 1991a), focused on the very question of the existential and ontological difference between the two temporal dimensions, according to which the passage from one to the other should take place by means of an immediate installation, *d'emblée*, as Bergson himself wrote. In the essay Deleuze highlights the connection of this conception with the new characterisations of the present as act and utility rather than existence, and of the past as inactivity and virtuality, as 'an immemorial or ontological Memory':

> There must be a difference in kind between matter and memory, between pure perception and pure recollection, between the present and the past ... We have great difficulty in understanding a survival of the past in itself because we believe that the past is no longer, that it has ceased to be. We have thus confused Being with being-present. Nevertheless, the present *is not*; rather,

it is pure becoming, always outside itself. It *is* not, but it acts. (Deleuze 1991a: 57)

Deleuze continues:

> The past, on the other hand, has ceased to act or to be useful. But it has not ceased to be. Useless and inactive, impassive, it IS, in the full sense of the word: It is identical with being in itself ... At the limit, the ordinary determinations are reversed: of the present, we must say at every instant that it 'was,' and of the past, that it 'is,' that it is eternally, for all time. This is the difference in kind between the past and the present. (Deleuze 1991a: 55)

This point, a memory which is always 'already there', is the focus of Alain Badiou's interpretation, according to which the existence of a self-preserving past determines in Deleuze's thought a 'de-temporalisation of time' that would make him an involuntary disciple of Plato. This time passing and yet eternal as ontological and virtual memory becomes truth itself, which Deleuze substitutes for the idea of truth understood as a normative and abstract category. The power of falsity as virtual Being is nothing other than the new name which Deleuze gives to truth, a truth which is the expression of the eternal and which the philosopher defends 'with gentle violence', in a reflection which Badiou defines classical as his own thought is classical (Badiou 1999). In this sense Deleuze is even compared to Hegel, because for both the 'sovereignty of the One' implies the idea of truth as the preservation of the immanent, as absolute past (virtuality for the former, concept for the latter). The divergence between the two reflections amounts to the structure of memory, which on the one side operates through differentiations and virtualisations, while on the other through firm steps, through 'monumental figures'.

However, besides the obvious acknowledgement of this gap, whose seminal importance has been admitted by Badiou himself, it should be noted that the differentiation through relation is for Deleuze much more than a modality of the memory, as it consists indeed in its structure, that is memory itself. Pure virtuality is in fact conceived as in continuous communication and incessant relation with the actual, with which it establishes an exchange enacting a qualitative transformation: it is eternal, inasmuch as it does not cease to exist, but not static, as it keeps changing. In this sense the present is both the actual image but also what moves on because a new present comes in, while the past is pure virtuality, related to its own present. In cinema the revelation of temporality in itself – shown in the crystal of the two streams of past and present constantly encountering, exchanging and splitting – gets displayed through the two chronic images which do not make reference to the series, but rather to the order of time: the former grounded in the past which gets preserved, existing for itself, and allowing the appearance of entire fields of memory, which Deleuze defines as sheets of the past; the latter is instead grounded in a deactualised present – already split in modern cinema by its sensory-motor extension – and becomes an ecstatic dimension subtracted to the actualising function of converting the recollection into action, using it as a response to the perceptual act.

The challenge here is that of appreciating the nature of the impulse enabling the passage to the virtuality in its irreducible ontological difference from the actual: it is surely not an intellectual or psychological process, but rather a dribbling or suspension of the habitual which forces time 'out of joint', as Hamlet said. On the other hand, if it is true that between the two dimensions – which are simultaneously indiscernible – there is a continuous short-circuit, then this disentanglement from actuality would never be absolute and complete. In his introduction to the Italian edition of Deleuze's essays on Bergsonism, individuating the two key words of his reading of the volume in the terms *difference* and *virtual*, Pier Aldo Rovatti insists on the exchange and on movement. He writes:

> The conjunction is essential; the 'and' which connects and mobilizes the virtual and the actual, since it is precisely this mobilization which confers to the virtual its character of reality. That 'coexistence' ... is once again the mark of the discharging of time operated by the virtual, and yet its difference is now recognizable as a complex movement of differentiation whose circularity allows us to glimpse the rhythm of a constant oscillation rather than the pause on a position (the virtual) or the other (the actual). (Rovatti 2001: xvi; my translation)

Note

1. The affirmation of the existence of a pure past in itself cannot but make one think of Proust's conception of time. However, Deleuze himself suggests the difference between Proust and Bergson, for whom the pure past, although existent and real, is not by any means a lived experience. See Deleuze 2000.

Modernity

I.

The notion of modernity, which Deleuze connects with the emergence after the second world conflict of a new kind of image, has actually been associated by scholars with the very origins of cinema, to note in the first place its 'late arrival' compared with other forms of artistic expression. This aspect is particularly evident in the theories advanced immediately after the invention of cinema, since it has been connected to the themes of the legitimacy of cinema as an art and of the position of the new device within a stable system, thus constituting a recurrent motif of the aesthetic reflection. To claim that cinema is the latest art in terms of appearance meant for the first theorists that, although dependent on a new technical invention and born as a predominantly amusing and recreational event, still the cinematographic event should be given its rightful place among the forms of artistic expression. If it is possible to individuate some typical paradigms of modernity emerging from the course of the various theories of cinema – cinema as a technical innovation, as a possibility of a new perception typical of the modern subject, as a mirror of contemporary society – Deleuze, by reformulating a distinction already in place in the reflection of André Bazin, envisioned a radically different theoretical and stylistic division between classical and modern (De Vincenti 1993: 19).[1]

According to this reading, the essence of modernity – a notion which in Deleuze's understanding does not have a merely historical-chronological connotation but rather a 'distinctive transcendental, trans-historical character' (De Gaetano 1996: 101; my translation) – got manifested in the urgency – felt in Italy after 1945 with neorealism, in the next decade in France with *nouvelle vague*, and in the following one in Germany – to abandon the classical narrative form. In this way we see in

Deleuze Studies 8.3 (2014): 342–353
DOI: 10.3366/dls.2014.0154
© Daniela Angelucci
www.euppublishing.com/dls

films the emergence of 'purely optical and sound situations', of images disconnected from perceptual connections and dislocated in an empty space, and a precise theoretical connotation. This new modality, which seems to offer a renewed autonomy to image itself, certainly has its social, economic and political causes, but embodies in the first place a different stylistic attitude of the film, which is not centred any more on the relationships of cause–effect and perception–action typical of the concatenation of events in classical narrative cinema. As already noted, the cinematographic regime of modernity gets associated with the possibility of an immediate presentation of the virtual and of temporality 'in person': whereas in classical cinema the progress of events was conveyed through the characters' activity, through movement, the new narrative way makes truth and falsity indiscernible from the very choice of the themes through the usage of – among other things – *décadrages* and false recollections.

The novelty in the cinematographic style of movements and authors of modernity has been already stressed, obviously, by scholars; it is worth remembering, for example, the pages of Bazin on neorealism, aimed at emphasising the distance of the new cinematographic form from the classical one. In his essay on the Italian school of Liberation, referring to Roberto Rossellini's *Paisà* (1946), the French critic highlighted precisely the difference between the two narrative logics: the modern, neorealist one in which the spirit of the spectator, facing the fragments of reality jumbled by an elliptic montage, should pass from one fact to the other 'as one jumps from rock to rock in order to cross the river', and the other of classical *découpage*, in which the facts engage with each other 'as a chain in a pronged wheel', as if they are 'at the service' of our imagination.[2]

The description that Deleuze advances at the end of the first volume on cinema conveys the manifest signs of the new image, which according to him threaten in various ways the system of action: the 'dispersive situation', an ensemble of uncertain and empty spaces; the 'deliberately weak links', not following a well-defined logic any more; the 'voyage form', in which space is experienced in a casual way; the 'consciousness of clichés', the awareness that a such a loosely cohesive world might find its unity only in the current clichés of the time; and the 'condemnation of the plot' (Deleuze 1986: 210), the revelation of the existence of an occult power feeding such clichés, which, by mixing up with its very same effects, cannot be confined.

In Rossellini's *Germany, Year Zero* (1948), a film in which all these features patently appear together, the child-protagonist is certainly more a 'seer' (*voyant*) than an 'agent' (*actant*); the child wanders in the dispersive reality of the devastated post-World War II Berlin menaced by the clichés of the time, and his suicide should be read as an extreme act of condemnation against such conditions. In France the *nouvelle vague* elaborated the features of neorealism in a reflexive direction by loosening up even further the sensory-motor bonds, creating a cinema of purely optical and sound situations in which objects, signs and acts are not functional to the scenic action anymore, but acquire autonomous value.

Among the many films one might mention, the symbol of the French *nouvelle vague* is the image of the face of Jean-Paul Belmondo covered with blue paint in the finale of *Pierrot le fou* (1965) by Jean-Luc Godard, a tale of the crazy journey of Marianne and Ferdinand-Pierrot, completely devoid of sensory-motor bonds: to the complete disorder of the narration and the rarefaction of the characters correspond the aesthetic fullness of each scene and the stylistic richness of a film which blends together analogical shots and digital video, ellipses, repetitions, citations, gazes in camera, and false connections. Deleuze comments:

> In these we see the birth of a race of charming, moving characters who are hardly concerned by the events which happen to them – even treason, even death – and experience and act out obscure events which are as poorly linked as the portion of the any-space-whatever which they traverse. (Deleuze 1986: 213)

II.

The difference between the two cinematographic regimes – classical and contemporary, organic and crystalline, of movement and of time – is articulated by Deleuze in the sixth chapter of *The Time-Image* along three registers: description, narration, and story. In the first place, from the *descriptive* point of view, organic cinema presupposes the autonomous existence of its own objects, independently from the depiction operated by the camera, in order to build a sensory-motor situation in which the character acts or reacts within the bounds of the circumstance he or she is experiencing. With the crisis of the action-image, description replaces what is being filmed, constituting itself the dismantled, created and cancelled object that the subject observes and registers but of which he or she is no 'agent' any more: the autonomy from a specific environment qualifies these objects as purely optical and sound situations, separated from any possible reaction and lacking any motor extension.

The existence of such bonds, of causal and logical connections obeying the rules of succession and simultaneity, guaranteed in classical cinema the continuity of that reality which was presupposed by, and which at the same time defined, the regime of the imaginary as its opposite pole, determined in contrast as the self-contained moment in which images would appear as incoherent and disconnected. The questioning of movement-cinema generated a novel relationship between the real and the imaginary, two ontologically different regimes which in the new kind of description constantly overrun each other to the point of becoming indiscernible. The perpetual exchange between the two dimensions is presented as an unbroken short-circuit, where the smallest circle – in which the actual, with its continuous and imperceptible oscillations, gets transformed without pause in its virtual and vice versa – represents the true essence of what Deleuze defines as the crystal.

III.

From a *narrative* perspective, in classical cinema the development of the linear scheme of perception–action guides the plot, which maintains in this way a presumption of truthfulness also in the presence of dreamlike elements or recollections in the montage, rendered through juxtapositions and ellipses. In this field of forces, corresponding to a Euclidean space, time is represented only indirectly because it derives from movement, and its flow is pictured through action: it is a chronological time. Once the sensory-motor schemes have been abandoned, modern narration gives life to characters moving into a pure optical situation in which the anomaly of movement becomes the rule and space is not organised according to Euclidean rules or determined paths any more. Deleuze writes:

> Now what characterizes these spaces is that their nature cannot be explained in a simple spatial way. They imply non-localizable relations. These are direct representations of time. We no longer have an indirect image of time which derives from movement, but a direct time-image from which movement derives. (Deleuze 1989: 129)

The general consequence of this immediate exhibition of temporality is that time in itself, chronic and no longer chronological, jeopardises the very concept of truth. What is at stake is not a simple version of content relativism, for which different opinions would correspond to different times, but rather the difficulty (for thought) of obtaining a direct connection between truth and the structure of time, as it emerges from the history of philosophy with the ancient paradox of the contingent futures. In the context of Leibniz's proposed solution to the paradox – according to which tomorrow something can take place or not in two diverse worlds, both possible but not 'compossible', so that it is the 'incompossible' (and not the impossible) which progresses from the possible, and the past can be true but non-necessarily so – Deleuze quotes Borges's *The Garden of Forking Paths* in order to claim the co-presence in the same world of incompossible elements, in a labyrinth of time in which the 'pasts' are not necessarily true. Deleuze writes that 'nothing prevents us from affirming that incompossibles belong to the same world, that incompossible worlds belong to the same universe' (Deleuze 1989: 131); and 'contrary to what Leibniz believed, all these worlds belong to the same universe and constitute modifications of the same story' (Deleuze 1989: 132). This is the norm of the new falsifying narration of crystalline cinema, which proposes and amplifies a modality of description in which the real and the imaginary are indiscernible, displacing the narrative veracity and the sensory-motor concatenation of movement-image.

Deleuze dedicates a chapter of *The Fold: Leibniz and the Baroque* (1992) to the Leibnizian notion of incompossibility: for Leibniz, the contradiction is not between Adam sinner and Adam not sinner, but rather between Adam not sinner and the world in which he committed sin. This exemplifies the new relationship that Leibniz calls 'incompossibility', and it is from among this divergent series of possible worlds, although incompossible between each other, that God would pick the best one. Deleuze quotes Borges again, who instead would like God to keep all incompossible worlds existing at the same time. The main difficulty is that, should he actually behave like that and thus violate the rules of his own game, God would become a mendacious, trickster, deceiving deity: we face once again the problem of the false (Deleuze 1992: 71).

On this theme Deleuze's examples are copious and captivating. The abandonment of a narrative striving for truth and the emergence of the forger characterise the whole work of Alain Robbe-Grillet: in particular, the protagonist of *The Man Who Lies* (1968) is not 'a localized liar, but an unlocalizable and chronic forger' (Deleuze 1989: 132). Among the films by Alain Resnais, Deleuze mentions *Stavisky* (1974) – perhaps not his greatest achievement, but rather the one which 'contains the secret of the others': the film revolves around an investor who built his wealth on frauds, thus unmasking a world which is in its turn deceiving. Pure descriptions and the bond between falsity and temporality are the underlying cipher of Jean-Luc Godard's work, of which in this context Deleuze mentions *The Big Swindler* (1964), inspired by an episode of Herman Melville's *The Confidence-Man*. This novel by Melville realised in literature precisely what the last book of *Zarathustra* accomplished in philosophy: the exhibition of a continuous and in-becoming series of forgers, presented through characters transforming and 'metamorphosing' into each other in a continuous shift, in which beyond each figure there always lies another. A great author of falsifying cinema is Orson Welles, whom we have already encountered as the director of *Citizen Kane*, and whom we will have the occasion to meet again.

The power of the false – not a criterion of evaluation or merit, but simply the intimate motive of modern cinema – becomes thus the general principle of the new cinematographic regime, capable of inspiring very different directors and in whose work it does not appear as a separated or self-contained moment but rather as the paradoxical foundation of all characters – including those traditionally striving for truth:

> So that investigators, witnesses and innocent or guilty heroes will participate in the same power of the false the degrees of which they will embody ... The truthful man will form part of the chain, at one end like the artist, at the other end, the nth power of the false. (Deleuze 1989: 133–4)

What is missing in this continuous postponement is the undeniable element at the base of every truthful narration and in general of the regime of movement built on action: namely, the system of judgement, that is, the possibility to identify a character and to individuate its coherent and bonding features. In the perpetual becoming of the new system, characterised by a plurality from which it is impossible to obtain any unity, the 'Ego = Ego' formula gets replaced by Rimbaud's 'I is another' formula.

IV.

Eventually, as regards the register of the *story* as well – that is, the relationship between subject and object, where objective stands for what the camera sees, and subjective for the point of view of the character – crystalline cinema unhinges the element of truthfulness, that is, the encounter of the two points of view, thus making impossible any definite and unmistakable identification. In the 'cinema of poetry' theorised by Pasolini the camera adopts, for example, an inside view, which simulates the manners and point of view of the characters in a mimetic relationship, so that the objective and the subjective images blend together and contaminate each other thus becoming indistinguishable. In his essay on the cinema of poetry of such authors as Antonioni, Godard and Bertolucci, Pasolini writes:

> The creation of a 'language of film poetry' thus implies the possibility of making pseudostories written with the language of poetry. The possibility, in short, of an art prose, of a series of lyrical pages ... The camera is therefore felt for good reasons. The alternation of different lenses ... etc. – this entire technical code came into being almost out of impatience with the rules, out of a need for an irregular and provocative freedom, out of an otherwise authentic or delicious enjoyment of anarchy. But then it quickly became the canon, the linguistic and prosodic patrimony that interests contemporary filmmaking the world over. (Pasolini 2005: 184)

Deleuze reprises Pasolini almost literally in his description of the style of modern cinema, neither subjective nor objective:

> The story no longer refers to an ideal of the truth which constitutes its veracity, but becomes a 'pseudo-story', a poem, a story which simulates or rather a simulation of the story. Objective and subjective images lose their distinction, but also their identification, in favor of a new circuit where they are wholly replaced, or contaminate each other, or are decomposed and recomposed. (Deleuze 1989: 150)

If Deleuze locates the origin of this change in Fritz Lang's as well as, once again, in Welles' films, this transformation of the subject–object connection is even more interesting in the cinematographic genre which more than any other aspired to the truth: namely, documentary and investigative films. This affirmation of a new will to storytelling, going beyond real and fiction, in direct and realistic cinema represents one of the most significant outcomes of the search for new expressive modalities. If the ideal of truth, sublimed by the selective and multiplying force of shots, was invariably tied to the cinematographic fiction from which it derived and on which it necessarily depended already in the masterpieces of the classical documentary cinema, in the 1970s investigative films – with the documentary films, shot in Quebec, by Pierre Perrault and the *cinéma-vérité* by Jean Rouch – tended to abandon the old schemes and get to the reality beyond the conditioning truth–fiction dichotomy as well. From the 1970s on, in fact, even in reportages and investigative cinema the relationship between the subjective and objective points of view underwent a progressive modification, aligning with *cinéma-vérité* in its search for an authenticity going beyond the truth–fiction dichotomy. A circumstance that exemplifies this cinematographic genre – in particular, Deleuze makes reference to Perrault and Rouch – is that in which the camera catches the characters in real and daily situations, but with the aim of showing their reaction to the camera's presence, which is emphasised so as to invite an interaction on their behalf. In this way the reality–fiction alternative becomes obsolete, because the authentic effect on reality as presented by the film is produced and created by cinema itself.

The goal of Perrault's criticism against fiction was the abandonment of the model of truth underlying it, the attainment of a pure 'storytelling function' through which a certain group, by re-telling itself, becomes other than itself without betraying itself and being false; the power of the false offers to the real character, as well as to the director, the possibility to invent, converting his or her story into 'the flagrant offence of making up legends'. Cinema should not fix the identity of a character, real *or* fictitious, through its objective and subjective aspects, but rather catch the becoming of the real character when he or she starts to 'make fiction' him- or herself, when he or she enters 'the flagrant offence of making up legends', contributing in this way to the invention of his or her own people (Deleuze 1989: 150–1).

In a similar way, the work of Rouch, who began with ethnographic reports from African countries and produced fictions starting with *Dionysos* (1986), can be labelled as *cinéma-vérité* since, by going beyond any pre-established ideal of reality to which fiction refers, it became the producer and creator of truth. The characters of Rouch – and the director as well, who through the use of an active and engaged camera becomes a character himself – in the unfolding of the simulating stories, and in the perpetual becoming other than themselves, form an image exceeding the confines of the present so as to catch the before and after, dimensions connected in a continuous transformation; what emerges here is the direct image of time in the form of unbroken becoming:

> The character must first of all be real if he is to affirm fiction as a power and not as a model: he has to start to tell stories in order to affirm himself all the more as real and not fictional. The character is continually becoming another, and is no longer separable from this becoming which emerges with a people. (Deleuze 1989: 152)

V.

At this point it should be noted how the distinction between modern cinema and classical regime – which, as we saw, we found already in Bazin – is reworked by Deleuze with a different emphasis, being the foundation of his entire theory of cinema, which he divided in the two volumes on the movement-image (the classical form) and time-image (the modern one), respectively. In *Film Fables* (Rancière 2006) Jacques Rancière questioned precisely the possibility of a neat distinction between the two ages of cinema. In the first place, Rancière does not see in the two modalities advanced by Deleuze two separate moments built in opposition, but rather two different points of view on images, united by an 'infinite spiral'. Rancière argues for this first basilar diversity in opinion by noticing the difficulty arising from the overlapping of the breaks in history and the ones internal to the image, that is, the attempt by Deleuze to envision an immediate connection between art and some of the events external to it. How is it possible, one might ask, to operate a classification about the kinds of sign by means of a heterogeneous factor? In regards to this first objection it should be noted right away that art and history represent different but not separate levels, and that the possibility of a repercussion of historical and political happenings on art can hardly be questioned, the more so from within a – convincing – conception such as Rancière's, who on more than one occasion theorised a strong bond between aesthetics and politics. In point of fact, in *The Politics of Aesthetics: The Distribution of the Sensible* (Rancière 2004) Rancière individuated in the artistic practices the visible forms of an organisation of the sensible, a 'partition' founded on the ways of life, on politics, and on the form of activities structuring the concept of citizenship.

Going back to the divide between classical and modern in cinema, which Deleuze defines in terms of two different logics of the image, it is for Rancière rather one taking place at the transcendental level: the very same images can be considered either from the point of view of a philosophy of nature, which examines them as material events, or from the point of view of a philosophy of spirit, which instead sees them as a form of thought, without assuming any breaking point pointing to the crisis of modernity. The potentialities of purely optical and sound situations of the time-image were already expressed in what Deleuze, in *The Movement-Image*, defined as the affection-image, that is, an image which, through the hesitation in the active response, gives rise to the predominance of the sensible qualities. This is demonstrated by the fact that certain authors discussed in the first volume return as an example of a new configuration of the image in the second; the example given by Rancière is Robert Bresson. According to Rancière, this notion of cinematographic image as a phase distinct from the classical age seems to be affected by the very same problems haunting modernism in general, with its affirmation of the autonomy of art as the manifestation of its peculiar essence. In fact, it conceals the complexity of what he defines as the passage, begun in the nineteenth century, to the aesthetic regime of arts, a regime in which 'the image is not the codified expression of a thought or feeling. It is rather the way in which things themselves speak and at the same time are silent' (Rancière 2009: 13). This enfranchisement from the mimetic requirement is guaranteed not so much by the liberation and autonomy of art from any representative pressure, but rather by the unity of the opposites exhibited in this kind of image: the unity of the pure passivity of things and the pure activity of creation. Cinema thus embodies the completion (and at the same time the confutation) of the aesthetic regime, uniting the passivity of the mechanical eye of the camera with the activity of the director as sovereign will:

> Cinema, due to its technical apparatus, literally embodies this unity of contraries in the union of the passive and automatic eye of the camera and the conscious eye of the director ... Unlike novelists and painters, who are themselves the agents of their becoming-passive, the camera cannot but be passive. In the cinema, the identity of contraries is there at the outset, and hence lost from the outset. (Rancière 2009: 117–8)

The necessity of a more elaborated vision of artistic modernity in general, in which the autonomy is achieved at the price of a contrast, and the unity of the opposites – activity and passivity – as the engine of cinema in particular, are certainly very important and fecund suggestions. For example, the definition of cinema as a 'countered fable', indicating a correlation between what is visible and what is sayable in terms of an interdependence, persuasively determines the debate on the topic 'cinema: visual or narrative art?' animating the first film theories (and which still animates the discussions in the Anglo-American analytic debate). The contrast between the two elements in the binary representative regime of cinema indicates, according to Rancière, that the visible element can manifest itself in all its breadth only by emerging from the plot, that is, by fighting with it, with the Aristotelian 'fable'. The power of the image shows itself as a 'gap', in collision with the narrative concatenation which becomes its antagonist, but also the necessary form for its emergence.

However, from this perspective there does not follow the impossibility of individuating a modern phase of cinema as Deleuze envisions it, keeping in mind firstly that in his writings the notion of modernity does not ever have a merely and rigidly chronological acceptance, if only in an extremely superficial understanding. Although its predominance can be appreciated starting from neorealism, the category of modernity explicitly acquires with its classical counterpart a trans-historical meaning – it suffices to think that *Citizen Kane* by Orson Welles, dated 1941, is indicated as the first film of the new regime of time. That the two texts on cinema do not aspire to constitute a history is explicitly stated by Deleuze at the start of the first volume, while what he means by classification can be clearly learned in a conversation which appeared in 1986 in *Cahiers du cinéma*, now collected in *Two Regimes of Madness*:

> There is nothing quite so amusing as classifications and tables. A classification scheme is like the skeleton of a book; it's like a vocabulary or a dictionary ... Every classification is similar: they are flexible, their criteria vary according to the cases presented, they have a retroactive effect, and they can be infinitely refined or reorganized. Some compartments are crowded, and others are empty. In any classification scheme, some things which seem very different are brought closer together, and others which seem very close are separated. (Deleuze 2006: 285)

Therefore, a classification is thus understood by Deleuze as an infinite and always unstable list. If it is true that each film – classical or modern – presents itself as a split and contrasted fable in which it the gap existing between the passivity of the mechanical eye and the purposiveness of the director's choice is noticeable, in the narrative concatenation of events and the force of the pure image of the cinema of a certain age we can acknowledge with Deleuze a predominant mark of freedom from certain schemes and of self-reflexivity without having the pretence of building a history of cinema on it, nor a rigid scheme within which each element should square with the other in a definitive way. The clues of this transformation of the image can be appreciated in the style of the direction – the camera movements, the rhythm and system of montage – but also in the interest in some recurrent themes and figures (the child, the invalid, the fool, the neurotic). These incarnations of an impossibility in the perceptual response, rather than necessary allegories – since, as Rancière writes, the rupture of the sensory-motor connections 'cannot be identified as an actual difference between types of images' (Rancière 2006: 116) – represent the signs of a deep-seated impotence and renouncement of action.

The roots of the distinction between the two kinds of image lie precisely in the emergence of a radically different dimension – that is, virtuality as time in itself – and in the abandonment of actuality – that is, dropping the Bergsonian terminology adopted by Deleuze, the idea that in modern cinema the situation and the characters exist independently from action, acquiring on the contrary their very existence from their being placed at the suspension of movement; that is to say, not simply overcoming the motor scheme, but rather by breaking it from within. This is also what Deleuze indicates as the difference between affection-image, the anchor internal to the organic regime of movement, and time-image: the hesitation featuring them discharges in one case in the plan of actuality while in the other through a complete immersion into memory. In this context the words of Maurizio Grande are once again of help:

> Deleuze is able to classify the affection-image as movement-image (and not as time-image) because in this case we have the indirect representation of the time of interiority through the interruption of 'edited' action. Close ups interrupt the progression of action and inscribe the duration of the expression of affection on a face inscribed in an anonymous space subtracted to any determinate space and to the indirect representation of time resulting from the montage. (Grande 2003: 386; my translation)

Going back to the Bergsonian language of *Matter and Memory*, in the case of affection we can speak of a hesitation in the response that does not provoke a 'leap' in memory, but rather stays in the sensory-motor present of mechanical recognition, while instead the time-image contemplates a search in the past animating perceptive recognition. Departing from a non-historic-chronological perspective, although descriptive and classificatory in the specific and paradoxical sense indicated by Deleuze, the identification of a tension internal to cinematographic art denoting its belonging to the aesthetic regime as the unity of contraries (the overlapping and interplay of two diverse attitudes) does not prevent the possibility of a new modern modality of the image, with its distinctive predominant character (both formal and related to its contents), and in which the virtual dimension becomes pre-eminent and directly exhibited.

Notes

1. Giorgio De Vincenti, in his volume *Il concetto di modernità nel cinema* (1993), focused on the theoretical line hailing from Bazin, individuating 'the combination of the meta-linguistic commitment with the recovery of the reproductive aspect' as its moving theme.
2. Rancière defined such a discrete character of images, which in modern cinema gain a certain aesthetic harmony by almost emerging from the narration and imposing themselves in their visual power, as the 'great parataxis' of modern cinema. See Rancière 2009.

Falsehood

I.

The question of falsehood, central to Deleuze's philosophy of cinema as already appreciated in the discussion of the difference between modern and classical cinema, animates the interpretation which he gives of the poetics of Orson Welles, an uncommon director with an overflowing personality on whom it is worthwhile to pause. The numerous interviews Welles gave during his career reveal a vital and contradictory character; the director generously offered himself to the camera, pronouncing on serious and substantive issues with self-confident nonchalance and without renouncing his taste for paradox. Always characterised by the magnitude of his style – aristocratic and yet anarchical, as he himself portrayed it – there coexisted different attitudes and reactions: the director appears authoritative with the young Peter Bogdanovich, who carefully gets prepared for their meetings for the book interview (Welles and Bogdanovich 1992);[1] he looks sincerely saddened even by the only partially negative reception of his work, which sometimes annoyed him; he is at times revengeful and occasionally elusive in revealing the well-known unlucky events related to the production of some of his films. Convinced of the primacy of the work over the author, Welles reveals at times a certain impatience for theoretical issues, as for example in his interviews with the cinematographic critiques of *Cahiers du cinéma*,[2] and he often downplays the importance attributed to the direction and to the methodology used.

Despite this plurality of behaviours and positions, or rather precisely because of the brilliant intertwinement of all these elements, there emerges a common trait representing the neatest cipher of Welles' personality and work: the love for life and for the existent, which the director fully enjoys and whose inevitable contradictions he consciously

Deleuze Studies 8.3 (2014): 354–364
DOI: 10.3366/dls.2014.0155
© Daniela Angelucci
www.euppublishing.com/dls

endorses. The indulgent treatment that Welles reserves for the contra-
dictoriness of reality – which is evident in his characters if it is true that,
to use the words Shakespeare gave to Hamlet to talk about dramatic
art, cinema should 'hold a mirror up to Nature' – does not surface only
formally, but it gets explicitly thematised several times. To Kenneth
Tynan, who asks him for clarification on the incompatibility of certain
assertions of his, Welles replies:

> For 30 years people have been asking me how I reconcile X with Y! The
> truthful answer is that I don't. Everything about me is a contradiction, and
> so is everything about everybody I know. We are made out of oppositions;
> we live between two poles. There's a Philistine and an aesthete in all of us,
> and a murderer and a saint. You don't reconcile the poles. You just recognize
> them.[3]

Welles' extraordinary ability to create, and in the majority of his
films also to interpret, remarkable negative characters, always animated
by a tender commitment, originates within this eternally conscious
acknowledgement of human duplicity and ambiguity. In fact, the
director 'chivalrously' offers to felons all the possible justifications
for their crimes, shrouding them in a tragic mist, preventing in this
way the spectator from elaborating a clear moral evaluation. The
publishing tycoon protagonist of *Citizen Kane* (1941) is a man abusing
his authority and wealth, but the public cannot but feel compassionate
for the character, combining the greatness of his endeavours with
the melancholy of the loser. The possibility of judging him is also
complicated by the fact that we are unable to decide who the true Kane
is, whether he is the one described by his protector, by his wife, by his
collaborator or by the butler. In *Othello* (1952) Iago certainly is the
traitor, whose treachery, as Welles says, finds no other reason than his
nature, but the same Othello is unable to understand the complexity
of reality, and the motive for his search for truth is hideous envy. The
plot of *Mr. Arkadin* (1955) consists in a continuous switch of roles,
all inspired by fiction: the billionaire Arkadin is approached by the
swashbuckler Van Stratten who wants to blackmail him, but who in
turn gets hired to reconstruct Arkadin's past, not because the latter has
completely forgotten it due to amnesia, as he wants others to believe, but
rather with the goal in mind of getting rid of the witnesses to his fault,
among whom, as will become clear at the end, there is the detective
himself.

In *Touch of Evil* (1958) all the leading characters are on closer
inspection morally dubious. Captain Quinlan, who uses false evidence

in order to frame the true culprits, has the moves and the appearance of a real felon, who however, by means of dishonest methods, operates in the service of justice: 'He was some kind of man. What does it matter what you say about people?', the ambiguous fortune-teller Tana, performed by an outstanding Marlene Dietrich, says about him after his death; Menzies, Quinlan's devout assistant, stages a plain betrayal, notwithstanding that his friend once saved his life; even the righteous agent Vargas, as Welles himself would remark in an interview, in order to reveal Quinlan's crimes obsessing him, does not hesitate to neglect his wife, exposing her and putting her in danger.

A plot full of tricks is also found in *The Lady from Shanghai* (1948), in which the seaman O'Hara falls in love with the wife of the wealthy lawyer Bannister, who hires him on their yacht leaving for the Caribbean; once back in San Francisco, the seaman – as a result of lies, shootings, and extortions – falls into Bannister's trap and is unjustly accused of the murder of his partner. The famous and visionary finale, in which O'Hara, eluding justice, assists the showdown between the billionaire and his wife Elsa (portrayed by a Rita Hayworth transformed by Welles into a dark lady far from the cliché of the Hollywood diva), which takes place in the mirror room of an amusement park, symbol of the multiplication of tricks and of the deformation of identities. In contrast to the films previously mentioned, here the director remarkably interprets the role of the positive hero, moralist and naive close to credulity. His last line, however, results in being meaningful and ironic, challenging with its jeering tone all the acquired certainties: 'I'd be innocent, officially. But that's a big word, innocent. Stupid is more like it. Well, everybody is somebody's fool. The only way to stay out of trouble is to grow old. So I guess I'll concentrate on that.'

The moral ambiguity of these figures staged by Welles – to mention only a few films in which the refusal to judge the characters is evident[4] – is an element that the critics have stressed since from his earliest works: François Truffaut remarked on it in an article on *Arts*, André Bazin in the *Observateur* and most importantly in the interview conducted together with Charles Bitsch and Jean Domarchi and published in *Cahiers du cinéma* in 1958, whose declared aim is that of 'discovering the ideal character recurring in all his films'.[5] Initially Welles tends to minimise the recurrence of a common trait in all his great interpretations: his personality as an actor is the cause of the predilection for a humanity *bigger than life*, majestic in its wickedness and often tragically defeated (the first three films mentioned, *Citizen*

Kane, *Othello* and *Mr. Arkadin*, open with the death of the protagonist). As an actor, Welles states that he feels the obligation to enrich with his better part the morally hideous characters he plays, to be loyal to the role he plays, for which he should offer the best justification. In this way, not without a certain delight in disorienting his interviewers, Welles begins the conversation manifesting his hatred for Quinlan, a 'despicable' man like Kane, for whom however – and here the subversion begins – one can feel sympathy and repugnance at the same time. In the same way, Arkadin is an opportunist born out of a corrupted world, of which he however represents the best possible expression, as his spirit is 'courageous and passionate'. In answering the many questions asked, the director reveals more and more, acknowledging that his condemnation is only intellectual, that is, conveyed only by thought and not by heart, admitting his disinterest, or even repulsion, for the rhetorical and sentimental values of bourgeois morality, in favour of an adhesion to life in all its aspects, of an aristocratic ethics:

[Generosity is] the chief virtue. I hate all the opinions which deprive humanity of the least of its privileges; if any creed demands that one should renounce something human, then I detest it ... I detest anyone who wants to cut off a note from the human scale; at every moment one ought to be able to strike any notes one desires. (Estrin 2002: 57)

It is only within this vision that one can thus appreciate the cipher of the Wellesian motif of *character*: not simply one's personality or temperament, but 'the way one behaves when one denies the laws one should obey, and refuses to act in accordance with the emotions one feels; it's the way one behaves in the face of life and death' (Estrin 2002: 74). The obvious reference is to the tale of the frog and the scorpion recounted in *Mr. Arkadin*: the frog agrees to carry the scorpion on her back beyond the river believing that the scorpion will not bite her as that would be illogical, given that in that case he would die as well; but the scorpion bites her anyway, drowning with her, because, as he replies, 'I can't help it, it is my character.' Welles plays with the possible interpretations of this fable each time someone mentions it in an interview, and if his interlocutor believed he or she had identified a 'scorpion' or a 'frog' in one of his characters, in most cases the director hastened to contest him or her or say, for example, that yes, it is true, the scorpion is a scoundrel, but, in the first place, it is the frog who behaves unwittingly. The sole certainty is the underlying conviction of this poetics, that is, once again the impossibility of reconciling contradictions, the acknowledgement of the ineluctability of human duplicity: if it is not legitimate to justify a morally biased action with the pure and simple exhibition of one's character, doing it implies some tragic and fascinating dignity and standing, a sort of heroism whose attraction is difficult to resist.

II.

The Nietzscheism of Welles, already noticed by Bazin, Bitsch and Domarchi, lies at the centre of Deleuze's reading of his cinema; he in fact expresses the cornerstone of Welles' critique of truth with a quick and penetrating formula: 'affect as immanent evaluation, instead of judgment as transcendental value' (Deleuze 1989: 141). Welles' aim is thus not that of facilitating the collapse of an entire system of judgement in order to establish a different evaluative criterion acting as the superior principle, but rather that of judging every being and every action 'in relation to the life which they involve': 'the good is outpouring, ascending life, the kind which knows how to transform itself, to metamorphose itself according to the forces it encounters' (Deleuze 1989: 141). As he writes in conclusion to his 1962 volume on the German philosopher, Deleuze imagined 'Nietzsche withdrawing his stake from a game which is not his own' (Deleuze 1983: 195), intending to replace the usual, mistaken interpretations – first of all the one of the will to power as a will to control – with the acknowledgement of the sense of Nietzschean philosophy in the affirmation of multiplicity, of difference, of becoming.

This 'joy of the diversity', the exhibition of an always innocent life – a theme which naturally is also profoundly Deleuzian and which culminates in the affirmation of an 'aesthetic of believing' (a 'need to believe in this world, of which fools are a part', Deleuze 1989: 173, a theme which I shall reprise later) – gets realised in the cinema of Welles as well. However, if the affinity between the director and Nietzsche has been highlighted since the 1950s, and the interpretation of the power of the false in Welles' cinema offered by Deleuze reprised by the critics, only a few of them stressed and deepened its most robust theoretical aspect and import, which is, as Alain Badiou writes in his monograph on Deleuze, the 'main road' to access the Deleuzian idea of truth and his theory of time.[6] If in classical cinema, in *The Movement-Image*, narrative time emerges through movement according to the linear perception–action scheme guiding the story as well as the characters, with modernity the true protagonist of film is time itself, conveyed through opsigns and sonsigns, purely optical and sound situations, descriptions completely disjoined from any relationship with action.

As we have already seen, in *The Time-Image* the difference between the organic regime, classical or kinetic (related to movement), and the crystalline one, modern or chronic (time-related), is reprised and specified by using three different registers: description; narration, that is, the development of the sensory-motor scheme; and the plot, that is, the elaboration of the subject–object relationship in the film. The chapter in which this survey is operated is titled 'The Powers of the False': if in these pages Deleuze stresses the connection between the exhibition of pure time and the questioning of truth, the renunciation of the pretence of a truthful narration to make space for the force of the transformation and becoming finds in the cinema of Welles a first and still unsurpassed example.

III.

The movie that Deleuze considers as the manifest of cinema as the power of the false is *F for Fake* (1975), the last film directed and presented to the public by Welles. *F for Fake* presents to the spectator as a sort of documentary, although a rather peculiar one. Using some material shot in Ibiza by François Reichenbach in 1968 for a never completed investigative film on the falsification of works of art, Welles blends the portraits of some characters connected in various ways to artistic fiction: Elmyr de Hory, forger painter theorising the indistinguishability of authentic paintings from false ones; his biographer Clifford Irving, an American reporter who authored a fake autobiography of Howard Hughes, a rather controversial figure in himself; Reichenbach himself, presented as an ex-art merchant who buys some imitations by de Hory. The insertion of some scenes filming the director in slow motion while mounting the film makes evident the reflexive character typical of post-documentarism, of which Welles has been an interpreter by imposing, as Adriano Aprà writes, 'the concept of literary cinema and together the one of *fake documentary*' (Aprà 2003: 368; original emphasis; my translation). In some interviews, refuting the over-simplifying label of documentary, Welles spoke in fact of this film as a 'personal essay', a 'free-form essay on fakery'; it thus consists in a filmed meditation 'in the first person singular',[7] whose true protagonist is the false and its relationship to art.

However – and this is the other necessary and complementary aspect of the overcoming of the alternative between truth and falsehood – the spectator should fully adhere and trustingly abandon him- or herself to the fiction, which is the true protagonist of the film: the very act of watching and believing in what is seen seems likewise to be a decisive theme, implied by the most noticeable of the entanglements between truth and lie. This is the sense of the episode on voyeurism inserted at the beginning of the film, interpreted by Oja Kodar and inspired by her novel *The Girl Watchers*, in which a charming and showy woman walks along the street followed by the stares of the men. Welles expects from the public an enchanted gaze, a suspension of the incredulity similar to the one experienced while attending the show of an illusionist. As he replies to Bogdanovich, 'To me, magic begins and ends with the figure of the magician who asks the audience, for a moment, to believe that the lady is floating in the air' (Welles and Bogdanovich 1992: 182): the Deleuzian *croyance*, the belief in the world, extends also to its deceptions.

In the first scene the director appears precisely in the shoes of an illusionist, introducing himself as a charlatan and announcing that the themes treated in the film will be trickery, frauds and lies,[8] joining from the very beginning the unbroken series of forgers he introduces as narrator and sarcastic barker. Also evoked in the course of the film are both his debut as actor at the Dublin Gate Theatre, where he was hired after lying about his alleged long experience as a star on the American stages of Broadway, and the launch of his Hollywood success, started 'with a flight into fakery ... by flying saucers' (Welles and Bogdanovich 1992: 182), thanks the radio trickery of *The War of the Worlds*. The only situation in which Welles reflects on his vision of art without any ironic tonality or mediation – in an atmosphere of nostalgia for a past time, a time before the separation between artist and artisan – is his monologue in front of Chartres cathedral, against which charm 'the juridical problem' of true and false annihilates in the aesthetic assessment: only the ugly is 'unauthentic' (Salotti 2000: 158; my translation). This extraordinary endeavour without signature is described by Welles in *F for Fake* as a 'rich stone forest' that, although perhaps will be demolished one day, now witnesses the mark of humankind and 'the anonymous glory of all things'.

The story of the false adventure of Oja Kodar as Picasso's model, ending with a fight between the painter and Oja's grandfather – who would have falsified the paintings for which she posed, destroying the originals – completes the chain of fakers. Welles intervenes again to disentangle this whirling twist of falsifications, once more in the role 'cosmopolitan hypnotist' (Deleuze 1989: 145): an hour before he promised to tell nothing but the truth while now, at the end of the film, he confesses that for the past seventeen minutes he has lied his head off, because reality – 'the toothbrush waiting home for you in its glass, a bus ticket, a pay-check, and a grave' – does not matter at all, and the only truth the professional liar ought to serve is art.

The richness and importance of the themes surveyed show that this film is neither the result of a new idea due to fortuitous circumstances,[9] nor a sheer 'adventure of the intellect, a flickering of paradoxes ..., an amazing labyrinth of mirrors' (Farassino 2004: 99; my translation), but rather a thoroughly poetical declaration in which all the themes most cherished by the director are displayed: illusion and magic, the primacy of the endeavour over its author – claimed in many interviews given to journalists and film critics – and also what Bogdanovich labelled as the pessimism of the Wellesian vision united with the optimism of his style, but above all the false and becoming, the trickery ousting the true and radically overturning its supremacy. Borrowing the words that Eric Rohmer dedicated to another work by Welles, *Mr. Arkadin* (Rohmer 1990: 137), under the eyes of the spectator a downright 'universal deception' takes place, in which truth and appearance result as inextricably entangled in a long and evolving chain of forgers: François Reichenbach, Elmyr de Hory, Clifford Irving, Howard Hughes, Welles, Oja Kodar and her grandfather, and Picasso himself. About the painter it is said in the film that, after having branded as fakes a number of canvases carrying his signature, he would have replied to those asking for the reason for his certainty that 'I can fake a Picasso just as well as anyone else'; what has gone missing is thus the idea of truth as a model to which falsehood contrasts as a copy, as an alternative. It is the affirmation of the negative, of difference in itself not ascribable to any identity, and Welles fully achieves all the transformations of crystalline cinema previously recalled: description substitutes action; the claim of narrative truthfulness is completely suppressed; identification results in being impossible, unresolvable.

Once the ideal of truth is deposed together with the world of appearances accompanying it as its correlate, what remains for Deleuze are power relationships among bodies, the influence of some powers over others, all nevertheless devoid of any unique and identifiable centre. The alternation between long sequence shots and fragmentary montage typical of Welles' films finds coherence, equilibrium and harmony precisely in the exhibition of the intensity of the different powers, filmed simultaneously in their relationships or singularly, in a fragmented succession so as to reproduce the multiplication of driving centres which were already displayed in the narrative plot or in the ambiguity of the characters. In the Wellesian work we witness for the first time the cinematographic mutation according to which linear movement built on an action core is replaced by an aberrant, anomalous movement which gets autonomy from its fixed structures, allowing in this way the liberation of time itself.

However, what is displayed in *F for Fake* as well as in the other films by Welles is not the total absence of a centre (which according to Deleuze is realised in the cinematography of Alain Resnais), but rather a radical metamorphosis of such a concept: 'The center ceased to be sensory-motor and, on the other hand, become optical, determining a new regime of description; on the other hand, at the same time, it became luminous, determining a new progression of narration' (Deleuze 1989: 140).[10]

The centre ceases to be a spatial and driving constant, and becomes in the first place a point of view, a glance from which the different filmed elements form a series in perpetual becoming. The succession of plain images within the short montage presents thus an alternation of descriptions and produces a concatenation and collection of different figures and aspects of the same character merging into each other. The other face of this 'architecture of vision' is instead a theory of shapes, in which the projection caused by a distant source of light marks and emphasises the volumes of the bodies and the connections among the multiple forces in play: it is the depth of field of Wellesian sequence shots.

In the end, in Welles' cinema we always have a single protagonist imposing him- or herself, that is, the forger exhibited in his or her transformations: the series of figures representing the metamorphoses of the false fastened to each other by treacheries and impostures, can be spotted from *The Lady from Shanghai* (in the 'infernal trio' composed of the attorney Bannister, the wife and her partner) up to the great series of characters in *F for Fake*. Here the collection of forgers is 'extensive and perfect', and ranges from 'the truthful man', who represents the premise for the very existence of the forger, his alibi, up to the artist himself, in whose creations the power of the false, the impossibility of distinguishing truth from mere appearance, is multiplied to the umpteenth degree. Differently from the common liar, the artist, who brings to bear the troop of fakers, does not get petrified nor crystallised in a figure of the metamorphosis 'acquiring a different form', but rather seizes the transformation itself, integrating it in the temporal perspective of becoming: the hoax becomes in this case a creation of something new. If for forgers, therefore, metamorphosis is restricted to their form of being, in art the thing in itself gets transformed in something new, 'because truth is not to be achieved, formed, or reproduced; it has to be created' (Deleuze 1989: 146). The artist – and this is the conclusion of Welles, Deleuze, but also of Nietzsche and Bergson – is the creator of truth.

With this sequence of evolving characters, which populate Welles' films as more or less elevated degrees of the will to power, is effected according to Deleuze a liberation of time from its subordination to movement, which finds its particular standing in the quality of becoming. We find here at work the second kind of chronosign, consisting in 'time as a series', that is, a succession which is not exterior, empirical or chronological any more, but rather intrinsic and chronological, in which 'the before and the after are not ... successive determinations of the course of time, but the two sides of the power, or the passage of the power to a higher power' (Deleuze 1989: 275). The series as a direct time-image has among its features that of questioning truth:

> The false ceases to be a simple appearance or even a lie, in order to achieve that power of becoming which constitutes series or degrees, which crosses limits, carries out metamorphoses, and develops along its whole path an act legend of story-telling. (Deleuze 1989: 275)

When movement loses its centre and becomes aberrant, thus encouraging the autonomy of time, the paradoxes coming to light – the impossibility of evoking the past, the emergence of an idle present, the union of a before and an after in perpetual becoming – impose a new logic which breaks up the order or the temporal series, thus making the ideal of truth collapse. This theme is connected with the Nietzschean pronouncement about the adhesion to *life* that will be the focus of the next chapter, which I shall introduce with the following long quotation from Deleuze's book on Nietzsche's philosophy:

> The activity of life is like a power of falsehood, of duping, dissimulating, dazzling and seducing. But, in order to be brought into effect, this power of falsehood must be selected, redoubled or repeated and thus elevated to a higher power. The power of falsehood must be taken as far as a *will* to deceive, an artistic will which alone is capable of competing with the ascetic ideal of successfully opposing it. It is *art* which invents the lies that raise falsehood to this highest affirmative power, that turns the will to deceive into something which is affirmed in the power of falsehood. For the artist, *appearance* no longer means the negation of the real in this world but this kind of selection, correction, redoubling and affirmation. (Deleuze 1983: 103)

Notes

1. In his introduction to the book collecting the interviews with the director from 1968–73, Bogdanovich recounts that Welles, when revising the text, modified not only his answers, but also sometimes the questions and the comments of his interviewer.
2. See the interviews to Welles by André Bazin and Charles Bitsch (*Cahiers du cinéma*, June 1958), and by Bazin, Bitsch and Jean Domarchi (September 1958), collected in Estrin 2002.
3. Interview by K. Tynan in *Playboy*, March 1967, now collected in Estrin 2002: 147.
4. The duplicity of the characters and the impossibility of judging them are also appreciable in other films by Welles beyond those mentioned. The deceit in judgement is, for example, the explicit protagonist of *The Trial* (1962), but also in this case Welles surprises his interviewers by showing his antipathy for K., very likely not responsible for what he is being persecuted for, but equally guilt, because he is an accomplice of the society in which he lives. Among the other greatly wicked figures it is worth remembering Harry Lime, a character in *The Third Man* (1949) by Carol Reed and portrayed by Welles, who contributed to the film, writing the dialogues. In the interview with A. Bazin, C. Bitsch and J. Domarchi, Welles declared about this issue that 'I wrote everything to do with this character, I created him all around' (Estrin 2002: 68); and continued 'I detest Harry Lime: he has no passion, he is cold; he is Lucifer, the fallen angel' (Estrin 2002: 71). For an account and an in-depth analysis of Welles' films, see Naremore 1978.
5. Interview with A. Bazin, C. Bitsch and J. Domarchi, in Estrin 2002: 51.
6. See Badiou 1999.
7. This is how Nepoti expresses himself in an essay titled 'Orson Welles: il cinema in prima persona' (2004), dedicated to *F for Fake* and to *Filming Othello*.
8. Before deciding on its definitive title, Welles pondered a number of titles, among which were *Hoax*, *Question Mark* and *Nothing but the Truth*.
9. The 1971 text *The 'Citizen Kane' Book* by Pauline Kael called into question the authorship of the script of *Citizen Kane* – which, by the way, was the only category of the film that won an Oscar despite being a candidate nine times with, among other things, best film, best director and best male actor in a leading role – attributing all the merit to the co-screenwriter Herman J. Manckiewicz.
10. Deleuze reprises here the analyses on the baroque by Michel Serres in his *Le Système de Leibniz* (1968). Through his depth of field Welles reproduced in the modern age the change in thought which took place in painting during the seventeenth century.

Life

I.

An overall view of the work of Gilles Deleuze discloses a strange but forceful coherence, an unexpected cohesion in a reflection open to multiple directions due to a continuous circulation of concepts, which, because they make reference to each other, result as invariably entwined. Among the issues informing virtually all his work is the recurring question about the nature of philosophy, which stands out in his two volumes on cinema as well. As we observed, if art creates sensible aggregates, characters, images and sounds, philosophy creates new concepts behind which there hide the questions and problems of a certain time. What is at stake is thus a conceptual practice which does not have to do, at least immediately, with truth and falsehood, a practice which is not abstract at all, but rather very concrete because it presents itself as a production, an invention of concepts meant to open a problematic space of discussion. Philosophy and art enter in this way into a mutual relationship of resonance with each other, not because one reflects upon the other, but rather for intrinsic reasons: both are 'sorts of separate melodic lines in constant interplay with each other' (Deleuze 1997a: 125). Philosophy does not retain any primacy in the reflective activity, and yet it does not suffer from inferiority for what concerns the act of creation.

If to philosophise means precisely to find the question, raising the problem and inventing always new concepts, the study of the history of philosophy represents thus a training, an apprenticeship in which, moving from the original concept created by a certain author, one goes back to the problem or issue that the new concept aims to answer. In commenting on philosophical texts one does not merely enact a double abstraction – that is, one does not reflect on the results of a previous reflection – but rather one engages in a philosophical portrait

Deleuze Studies 8.3 (2014): 365–374
DOI: 10.3366/dls.2014.0156
© Daniela Angelucci
www.euppublishing.com/dls

(once again the analogy with art and painting comes to view): a mental and conceptual portrait which does not reproduce what a certain thinker said, but rather explicates what he or she suggested, the unsaid implicit and present in what is said. However, it is also true that we read authors when we share with them the urgency of a problem, when we share the originality of a concept, as witnessed in Deleuze's usage of Bergson; as a result of this, there is thus no difference between philosophy and the history of philosophy.[1] In fact, in his work Deleuze never ceased to comment on other authors and at the same time, in doing so, convey his own personal and original thought.

Among the authors sharing a common cause with Deleuze we find Nietzsche, the philosopher of immanence together with Spinoza, a thinker who fought any transcendental principle. One of the 'zones of indiscernibility' between their thoughts – together with that of philosophy just mentioned – is the concept of life as inorganic power, a becoming force which incessantly struggles to overcome itself and at the same time a relationship between these elements. Once again this is a theme suffusing Deleuze's entire work, echoing and engaging many other aspects in a short-circuit which gives to its speculative movement the particular coherence just mentioned: suffice to remind that his last writing, *L'Immanence: une vie . . .*, is dedicated precisely to the idea of an indeterminate life, a life free from any individuation. However, I would like now to focus on a 1962 text by Deleuze dedicated to Nietzsche; a text which first of all takes credit for having inaugurated a new literature on the German philosopher in France, dismantling the interpretative habits of the previous decades.[2]

II.

The Deleuzian literature on Nietzsche starts from the reprisal of the now forgotten Pre-Socratic unity of thought and life, an overall unity in which life activates thought and thought affirms life. As Deleuze would write very clearly in the introduction to his 1965 anthology of Nietzschean studies (available in English in the collection Deleuze 2001):

> We now have only instances where thought bridles and mutilates life, making it sensible, and when life takes revenge and drives thought mad, losing itself along the way. Now we only have the choice between mediocre lives and mad thinkers. (Deleuze 2001: 66–7)

The loss of this overall unity of active life and affirmative thought is perspicuously introduced and explored in his earlier book on Nietzsche, in which the attempt to free the German thinker from any dialectical reading as well as the recognition of the core of his philosophy in the pure affirmation of becoming are achieved by making use of the Nietzschean notions of sense and value.

If for Nietzsche consciousness is only the symptom of a deeper transformation, of the unconscious activity of those forces which does not belong to the spiritual order, the sense of a phenomenon, an object, a body, is represented by the quality of the power necessary to take it over by dominating another power of a different sign. The relationship among the powers in play has nothing to do with an idle body, as the latter never configures itself as something neutral, but rather it represents a force submitting to the one, among the conflicting forces, most akin to its sense. Nietzsche does not negate the essence of a phenomenon, but rather he derives it from its affinity with the forces controlling it: the question of 'what?' gets replaced by the question of 'who?', which asks in the first place about the dominant forces, understanding phenomena as symptoms of their underlying forces. A body would thus be the result of a domination, an 'arbitrary product' whose unity is determined by the relationship between dominant and dominated forces. Envisioning an equivalence among the two forces, believing that their encounter might generate an equal result, is an illusion which according to Nietzsche characterises science, because the essence of a force lies precisely in the difference of quantity between the two forces originating it, in the result of their encounter: as Deleuze would put it, it is the differential element constituting its quality. There are thus active, affirmative forces – which when pushed to their extremes affirm their difference – and reactive, negating forces – which are able to dominate the active ones not by constituting a bigger force, which would acquire in its turn an active quality, but rather by acting through decomposition, that is, by separating the active force from what is in its power and involving it in the reaction.

In his *Bios. Biopolitica e filosofia* (*Bios. Biopolitics and Philosophy*, 2006), Roberto Esposito examines the Nietzschean will to power as a continuous 'strengthening of life', and investigates the relationship between the forces and the activity of the reactive forces 'draining it from within', separating it from itself. According to the author, in Nietzsche's philosophy the modern immunitary dynamic of 'the negative protection of life' figures in two different ways: as a process against whose contamination Nietzsche warns us to protect ourselves – since what allows life's conservation is also what blocks its expansion – but also as a process of decay that should be promoted and hastened in order to free the field to new affirmative forces. In Deleuze's reading there does not seem to take place any irreducible conflict between these two attitudes, because the triumph of affirmative forces, the necessary outcome of the history of nihilism itself, consists in a complete reversal which does not take place piecemeal or gradually, but rather through a transmutation of values: the negative to endorse is the one which becomes active, aggressive, joyful.[3]

In *The Genealogy of Morals* Nietzsche individuates the triumph of the reactive forces in history in the figures of resentment, bad consciousness and ascetic ideal, an ideal which inevitably allies with nihilism by devaluing existence and the mundane world through the fiction of a super-sensible world and values higher than life; the hatred for life results in a love for the exhausted, sick life in which what gets expressed is the will to nothing. But the ideas of good and the divine presiding over this moral and religious conception are accompanied, in the perspective of reaction, by the idea of truth typical of the speculative situation which Nietzsche radically criticises: it is from this excessive interest of thought for the reactive forces that derives the pretence, usually expressed by philosophers, that human beings strive for truth. Actually, the truthful person seeks truth because of being moved by completely different reasons, by

> something more profound: 'Life against life'. He wants life to become virtuous, to correct itself and to correct appearance, for it to serve as the way to the other world. He wants life to repudiate itself and to turn against itself. (Deleuze 1983: 96)

The conflict between knowledge and life and the contraposition of the two worlds, the one sensible and the other transcendental, thus reveals their essential moral nature: the favourite activity of the seeker of truth 'is the distribution of wrongs, he renders responsible, he denies innocence, he accuses and judges life, he denounces appearance' (Deleuze 1983: 96). Thought, on the other hand, should not be informed by truth understood as an abstract universal, but rather by the elements of meaning and value originating from it. Since from the essence of what is human necessarily follows its complicity with reactive forces, so that the presence of active forces has the only function of fostering the 'universal becoming-reactive', in order to enact a transmutation of value Nietzsche reflects on the Overman, not a human capable of surpassing himself, but rather one other than human.

According to this reading, the first misunderstanding to discard is the one regarding the will to power, which represents the genetic element of force, the internal completion giving it meaning and value, a flexible principle inseparable from force but not identical with it. The will to power is thus not a will to control, because the will, being the very source of values and admitting no external and pre-constituted end, cannot aim at control. On the same lines, Deleuze refutes the previous interpretations of the other key Nietzschean concept of eternal return as a cycle, a return of the same, resulting in a final state allegedly identical to the initial one.

According to Deleuze, the eternal return is in the first place a cosmological doctrine implying the affirmation of pure becoming, that is, the critique of the possibility of its final stage, from which the cycle of time should commence: if becoming were meant to become something, then it would have already done it. Since instead there does not exist any being contrasting becoming in itself, there is a being of becoming itself, which is precisely the return. Second, the eternal return works as an ethical and selective principle of the will to power, on the basis of the formula according to which 'whatever you will, will it in such a way that you also will its eternal return'. This affirmation of the will, a will which desires and bears the repetition and the return of the object of its affirmation, allows thus the transmutation of value, of the reactive forces into active ones, reaching the destruction – affirmative and not reactive – of nihilism: through the eternal return negation is actively negated and 'something comes into being which cannot do so without changing nature' (Deleuze 1983: 71). Eternal return reproduces a becoming that cannot but be active, being the 'yes' that the world says to itself, the cosmic expression of the Dionysiac spirit.

From this philosophy of will and of power derives the other Nietzschean concept deeply felt and shared by Deleuze: the innocence of existence as becoming. If each force is inseparable from what is in its power, the relationship among forces is characterised in the first place as non-guilty, that is, as radically innocent:

> We create grotesque representations of force and will, we separate force from what it can do, setting it up in ourselves as 'worthy' because it holds back from what it cannot do, but as 'blameworthy' in the thing where it manifests precisely the force that it has. We split the will in two, inventing a neutral subject endowed with free will to which we give the capacity to act and refrain from action. (Deleuze 1983: 23)

The most profound sense of Nietzschean philosophy understood as the affirmation of becoming consists not only in acknowledging that life is becoming, multiplicity and chance, but also in accepting and affirming it: the real virtue does not consist in renouncing each passion but rather in embracing them, saying 'yes' to life and to the world. For this reason, Deleuze's admiration for Kant, who invented many new concepts, led the French philosopher to the refutation of his 'system of tribunals'. Deleuze substitutes the judgement based on the value that transcends life, as if life were a sin to expiate, with an immanent evaluation carried out on the base of vital exigencies, which are in themselves innocent.

In *Essays Critical and Clinical* (1998) Deleuze dedicates an essay to the question of judgement; through the work of four authors – Nietzsche, Lawrence, Kafka and Artaud – Deleuze thematises a way of existence without judgement that, although not explicitly referred to the cinema of the time, finds in the incessant novelty of its creation the characters of pure description and of falsifying narration:

> What disturbed us was that in renouncing judgment we had the impression of depriving ourselves of any means of distinguishing between existing beings, between modes of existence, as if everything were now of equal value. But is it not rather judgment that presupposes preexisting criteria (higher values), criteria that preexist for all time (to the infinity of time), so that it can neither apprehend what is new in an existing being, nor even sense the creation of a mode of existence? Such a mode is created vitally, through combat, in the insomnia of sleep, and not without a certain cruelty toward itself: nothing of all is the result of judgment. Judgment prevents the emergence of any new mode of existence ... Herein, perhaps, lies the secret: to bring into existence and not to judge. (Deleuze 1998: 134–5)

The loss of any centre is associated with the disappearance of the system of judgement, irrevocably lost in the perpetual becoming which erupts as vital force, not truthful but rather falsifying. What remains is not a centre with its confronting forces, but rather the connections of the various forces at play, each referring to the others and inseparable from them.

The practical side of this speculative project – that is, the affirmation of the manifold which Deleuze obviously welcomes – consists in feeling the joy of the diverse, having the aesthetic form of the tragic in which any form of anguish or nostalgia for something lost is replaced with the joyful acceptance of plurality and of difference: 'tragedy (is) frank, dynamic, gaiety' (Deleuze 1983: 18), and Dionysus 'is the god for whom life does not have to be justified, for whom life is essentially just' (Deleuze 1983: 16). In *Time-Image* (a book which is Nietzschean as much as Bergsonian) the vindication of an ethics of joy translates – as already said – into the affirmation of an aesthetic of *croyance*, of faith: the need for 'Christians or atheists' to make the world an object of belief. If – as clearly appears in modern cinema, with its errant characters and disconnected spaces – the link between us and the world is broken as we are no longer organically and necessarily related to life, we need to substitute this disrupted link with faith, with the belief in 'this world, of which fools are a part' (Deleuze 1989: 173), and not in any transcendental dimension. Once the link between perception and reaction featuring the film of the classical regime is severed, cinema conveys the fragility of individuals, not agent but rather seer, facing something intolerable and unthinkable which, however, does not present as an exceptional event, but rather as a daily banality. As Deleuze writes, we should thus 'make use of this powerlessness to believe in life, and to discover the identity of thought and life' (Deleuze 1989: 170), that is, that identity which according to Nietzsche represents the Pre-Socratic secret par excellence.

The reactive judgement accusing life and its multiple becoming finds expression not only in ethics and religion, but in knowledge itself, which Nietzsche accuses of opposing vital values, considering itself as an end or offering its services to the reactive forces. Only a critique of knowledge would give new meaning to thought, making it affirmative, capable of following the vital forces to their extreme limit, so that thinking would be equated to the creation of new possibilities of life. The affinity between thought and life, concealed by a reactive understanding of knowledge, is guarded instead by art, in which takes place a sane rather than a sick will to power, totally free from the ascetic ideal. Deleuze's reading highlights two aspects of the tragic conception of art typical of Nietzsche: the vindication of an aesthetic of creation and the concept of art as the power of the false. In the first place, Nietzsche opposes the philosophical tradition that runs from Aristotle to Schopenhauer passing through Kant, for which art would be a disinterested activity. By observing art from the point of view of the artist, it would rather appear as 'a stimulant of the will to power'; the vision of a work of art does not comfort, purify or sublimate, but rather energises the will enacting the vital and active forces of the artist. If vital activity, which deceives and seduces, is akin to the power of the false, in art falsehood gets affirmed, doubled, elevated to the highest degree, making the artist a creator of new possibilities of life on par with the thinker. The power of the false is thus able to inspire very different authors and works, but the first director who endowed the image with the power of the false is, as already observed, Orson Welles, whose cinema is dominated by one kind of protagonist, the forger, exhibited in his or her various transformations. If the Nietzscheism of Welles is manifested in the first place in the perpetual critique of truth, it clearly appears also in his refusal (obviously connected to the first aspect) of the system of judgement, revealed in the extraordinary capacity to create magnificently wicked – and often tragically and gloriously loser – characters without committing to any moral evaluation, and indeed always inspired by a tender adhesion to life.

III.

One can ask at this point, what are the consequences of this adhesion to life? The Deleuzian classification of direct time-images – coexistence with the past, simultaneity of the peaks of the present, future becoming as creation – introduces, in the second volume on cinema, the big theme of cinematographic practice: namely, the relationship with thought. The automatic movement of the image (aspired to by all arts but achieved only by cinema) is able to 'communicat[e] *vibrations to the cortex, touching the nervous and cerebral system directly*' (Deleuze 1989: 156) generating a total shock to thought. This 'noochoc' (a 'barbaric' and traumatic word, designating the philosophical invention of a concept) is not characterised as a mere logical possibility, but rather as a power forcing us to think, reactivating in us a 'spiritual automaton', an automatic subjectivity able to push thought itself to its limit.

In movement cinema the image was thought as an organic totality, as a dialectical unity built around the constitution of its parts; thought was integrated in the image, shaped as a circuit, an open spiral comprising the film, the director, and the spectator. We thus have a sensory-motor unity in which the image and the concept are connect in a Hegelian way, and which represents the relationship between persons and the world, human beings and Nature, individuals and masses. According to Deleuze, in classical cinema all the modalities of the relationship between image and thought are in place in the work of Eisenstein, in which he individuates an organic moment (from perception to the concept), a pathetic one (from the concept to affection), and a dramatic one (in which image and concept coincide). However, for Deleuze the greatness of cinema as the new thinking and art of the masses ended up not only in the mediocrity of some productions, but most importantly in propagandist manipulation, which 'brought together Hitler and Hollywood, Hollywood and Hitler' (Deleuze 1989: 164): totality transforms into totalitarianism.

The occasion to abandon this phase is not offered by a renewed strength of thought, but rather by its lack, by a vacuum: the revelation of a constitutive impotence situated in its centre as an inability, an impossibility to think. Departing from the cinematographic experience and the writings of Antonin Artaud, Deleuze describes in fact a modernity that is unable to vindicate the unity of being and knowing, but only the difference, the interstices, the breaches, and a cinema forcing individuals to face the unthinkable. The films of purely optical and sound situations showed something that can be seen but not thought precisely because they have a seer character as the protagonist, deprived of any sensory-motor reaction. The way out of this sort of paralysis is for Deleuze an utterly moral choice, a wager almost à la Pascal. The absence of a unitary wisdom leads thought to belief, to the need of Christians and atheists to make the world an object of faith, given that we are not connected to it by an organic and necessary relationship. The Nietzschean model, by replacing wisdom with faith in the world in which we live, represents once again the end point of an idle thought.

Within the system of belief, the image of modernity develops a strong bond with the body, with its daily or ceremonial attitudes and stances representing life and the forces resisting the great categories of thought. 'Give me a body then' is the formula of a certain kind of cinema (Bene, Antonioni, Godard) built around the couple posture–voyeurism, finding its opposite pole – 'Give me a brain' – in intellectual cinema. The latter, as concrete as physical cinema, displays the cerebral mechanisms (Resnais, Kubrick), replaces the corporeal affections with the mental landscapes, which become 'our problem or our illness, our passion, rather than our mastery, our solution or decision (Deleuze 1989: 212). In fact, with the disappearance of the classical representation of the mind as interiority and harmonious totality, the determination of the cerebral activity by integration, differentiation and association necessarily fails; in this context interruptions acquire absolute value and are reproduced in modern cinema as loose images occupying the place left free by the system of movement.

The very evolution from classical to modern cinema reverberates in the issue of sound, which for Deleuze is not a separate element added a posteriori to the image, but rather a new component which radically transforms the image itself. Within the sound system – also comprising music, sounds as well as noises – words act as the herald of this shift, representing the sphere of sociality. If in the earlier phase of spoken cinema the verbal act was essentially interactive, concerning the relationship between two subjects, in the films in which the story is narrated by an out-field voice it becomes reflexive, and eventually autonomous when, free from any visual bond and even from the invisible one of the external narrator, it becomes itself the object of an autonomous framing. When the two movements of the image become reciprocally autonomous and indispensable, and the verbal act becomes itself an act of creation, the audio-visual image originates, which marks a third period in the story of cinema after silent and spoken cinema. In its last transformation, due to aesthetic and then technological causes, the image, become digital, is a sort of tableau of information, a spurt of information skating the surface, constituting and dissolving into other images.

Once again this is the passage from one system to another, from an indirect representation of time to its transcendental presentation in modern cinema, which in conclusion to his book – after having tackled the issue of sound and mentioned the birth of the information-image – Deleuze labels as a central moment for his theory. A theory which fiercely resists the charge of being abstract, defined by Deleuze as a practice related to others, and in this case to cinema.

Notes

1. Deleuze tackles this issue at length in the video-interview with Claire Parnet (Deleuze 1997b).
2. See Vattimo 2005: 146–7 and Vozza 2006: 146–51.
3. See Esposito 2006, and in particular chapter 3 on Nietzsche, in which the Deleuzian interpretation is mentioned as well.

Repetition

I.

As its very title suggests, at the origin of the 1968 volume *Difference and Repetition* we find the intertwinement of two lines of research: the first investigating a concept of difference free from negation, that is, a difference which is not a difference from, which is not opposed to anything, but which in its being unrelated to any model is rather autonomous and not subordinated to the identical. In this sense, later in the book Deleuze will speak of the simulacrum, the reflection or double described as a copy, however lacking any identity to the thing it refers to: 'not [a] simple imitation but rather the act by which the very idea of a model or privileged position is challenged and overturned' (Deleuze 1994: 69). Deleuze's project is thus that of subtracting difference from its 'state of malediction', that is, making it thinkable in itself without predicating it on something else and mistaking the copy for the original; a project of overturning Platonism which should necessary undergo a substitution: the replacement of generality and equivalence with *repetition* understood as the elevation to power, as the always novel affirmation of singularity.

We thus reach the second line of research of the text: the advancement of a concept of repetition in which all 'bare' repetitions, mechanisms and stereotypes might find their logic, as if repetition constituted the hidden structure of an always 'differential' criterion. There is a substantive difference between repetition and resemblance. In the former the singularities constituting the series are not interchangeable: it is not a matter of adding a second, a third or a fourth instance, but rather of bringing each time the first instance to the nth power. In repetition there takes place a variation, a 'modification' in which we can trace its automatisms and compulsions as well. In short: according to Deleuze

Deleuze Studies 8.3 (2014): 375–382
DOI: 10.3366/dls.2014.0157
© Daniela Angelucci
www.euppublishing.com/dls

these two directions – repetition and difference – cannot but join forces so that repetition as the affirmation of (pre-individual) singularities defines the proper working of difference.

According to Deleuze, from this point of view it is possible to draw a connection between Kierkegaard and Nietzsche. The unbridgeable gap between Kierkegaard's God and Nietzsche's Dionysus, indeed a hardly arguable distance, makes their convergence on the theme of repetition even more momentous. In fact, both oppose repetition to all forms of generality. Kierkegaard relates repetition to a selective test, making it the supreme object of the will and of freedom, specifying that it is not a matter of drawing something new from repetition, but rather of making repetition as such a novelty. Extracting something new from it would consist in fact in a contemplative, reflective act implying a meditation, whereas renewing repetition itself by reaffirming one's choice is an action, an affirmative performance.

If Deleuze shares with Nietzsche more than a common cause, we witness here once again the staging of the theme of the eternal return, which consists precisely 'in conceiving the same on the basis of the different' (Deleuze 1994: 41). With Nietzsche the eternal return becomes a formal law overturning Kantian morality on its very field. The maxim becomes: 'whatever you will, will it in such a manner that you also will its eternal return' – a maxim in which repetition literally substitutes universality. If making repetition the very object of the will means getting free from what enchains us, Deleuze insists on the fact that what enchains us is without doubt repetition itself. The existence of the same, the alike, the mechanical and for us oppressing repetition of the 'chain' is neither negated nor ignored; simply enough, it is only by moving from these premises that it is possible to find a principle of differentiation, since 'if we die of repetition we are also saved and healed by it – healed, above all, by the other repetition' (Deleuze 1994: 6). Such repetition that saves us consists in a choice, a selective act, the staging of an element which results each time in being shifted, masked and different without there being any prototypical principle or ultimate term of the series: 'The whole mystical game of loss and salvation is therefore contained in repetition, along with the whole *theatrical game* of life and death and the whole positive game of illness and death' (Deleuze 1994: 6; my emphasis).

One might ask, where does this strange closeness between Kierkegaard and Nietzsche come from? Both are interested in movement, says Deleuze, a movement based on novelty as opposed to the idea of an abstract logical movement, that is opposed once again to mediation.

Both substitute in fact mediated representations with direct signs: the leap for the former and the dance for the latter. This non-mediated movement, which does not move through opposition but rather directly, is repetition. As Kierkegaard affirms in *Fear and Trembling*: 'I only look at movements' (Kierkegaard 1986: 67), to which Deleuze comments: '[this] is the language of a director' (Deleuze 1994: 9). This idea of a theatrical game, of dramatisation, of direct presentation, is in fact a feature of philosophy but above all of art; it is at bottom what unites art and philosophy understood as inventive practices of sensible aggregates or of concepts. Both Kierkegaard and Nietzsche, writes Deleuze, invented for philosophy 'an incredible equivalent of theatre' (Deleuze 1994: 8), a theatre made of those conceptual characters which are the product of the philosophical practice itself.

In the conclusion of the book, after speculating about the coexistence between mechanical and hidden repetition, Deleuze arrives precisely at a characterisation of art:

> Perhaps the highest object of art is to bring into play simultaneously all these repetitions, with their differences in kind and rhythm, their respective displacements and disguises, their divergences and decentrings; to embed them in one another and to envelop the one or the other in illusions the 'effect' of which varies in each case. Art does not imitate, above all because it repeats; it repeats all the repetitions, by virtue of an internal power (an imitation is a copy, but art is simulation, it reverses copies into simulacra). (Deleuze 1994: 293)

At the beginning of *Difference and Repetition* Deleuze commenced his investigation exactly from art, characterising both the unconscious and art as two manifold fields each endowed with 'a power peculiar to repetition' (Deleuze 1994: xix).[1]

II.

Granted that both the unconscious and art possess *each its peculiar power of repetition*, is it possible to imagine an encounter between the two? That is to ask: once the Deleuzian conception of creativity and the Freudian idea of the unconscious are acknowledged, is it possible to envision a point of contact between these authors over the theme of repetition? Despite the fact that in *Difference and Repetition* Deleuze criticises Freud for his use of the compulsion to repeat – a bare, mechanical and non-differential repetition – as his primary theoretical element, I think it is possible to trace such a connection. My goal is not that of picturing a Deleuzian Freud, nor of establishing who is right, but rather that of investigating the possibility of endorsing a psychoanalytic perspective in aesthetics and in the reflection on art in general and cinema in particular, which does not endorse a symptomatic approach emphasising content over form, but rather one attentive to procedures and formal modalities. To put it in a nutshell: thinking aesthetic experience as an always different point of view on the same, a staging, a repetition employing formal processes and structures on which psychoanalysis can tell us something interesting.

In his 1914 'Remembering, Repeating and Working-Through' (Freud 1958: 147–56), Freud asserts that the first goal of the psychoanalytic technique is that of filling some memory blanks by overcoming the resistances caused by repression: *remembering*, being the chief goal of psychoanalysis, does not fill by chance the principal dominant position it does in the title. Freud observes soon after that, very often, we deal with a recollection that could not have been properly forgotten, as it was never conscious, never being present to consciousness.

If in the hypnotic method the progress of the act of recalling was simple, separated from the rest, with the application of the new psychoanalytic technique the patient does not recall the elements removed but rather puts them to work, reproducing those very elements not as recollections but rather as actions: she repeats them without being aware of it – for example, she does not claim to recall being hostile towards her parents' authority, but rather she puts to use this dynamic with the therapist from the very beginning of the treatment. The compulsion to repeat represents her way of recalling, through staging the removed elements. The bigger the patient's resistance is, the greater the intensity with which the recalling is substituted by this staging, by this repetition of the same.

Freud's conclusion is thus that, although it is always better to remember, still repetition represents the beginning of the cure:

> We render the compulsion harmless, and indeed useful, by giving it the right to assert itself in a definite field. We admit [the transfer] into the transference as a playground in which it is allowed to expand in almost complete freedom ... The transference thus creates an intermediate region between illness and real life through which the transition from the one to the other is made. (Freud 1958: 154)

Repetition is thus at the same time the illness from which we necessarily depart, and the mode of treatment available to us. This repetition in a monitored setting takes place in transfer understood as exercise, gym, implementation and staging. We are dealing with an active repetition, and not a passive movement (in fact, it has to be acknowledged, it is not enough to be aware and informed about one's own compulsion), and this same which we implement by returning to it is exactly a repetition in another environment, a repetition of the same from another point of view (perhaps with some degree of choice involved in the process).

Another place where Freud tackles this theme is his 1920 essay 'Beyond the Pleasure Principle': in this case it seems harder to relate repetition to a differential element because Freud here presents the compulsion to repeat as a manifestation of the inertia proper to the living organism, as the expression of the conservatory nature of living, the impulse to restore an ancient situation and thus the inanimate condition. However, the presentation of the *Fort-Da* advanced in this text tells us much more than that: the eighteen-month-old boy (Freud's nephew) he had the occasion to observe while repeating the game of making the wooden reel disappear (accompanying the gesture with a *'Fort'*, 'go away') and sometimes, but not always, making it reappear (greeting it with a joyful *'Da'*, 'there'), staging in this way the disappearance of his mother (and sometimes, but not always, her comeback), felt the pleasure of being able to dominate a situation which he previously only suffered. Freud writes:

> At the outset he was in a *passive* situation – he was overpowered by the experience; but, by repeating it, unpleasurable though it was, as a game, he took on an *active* part. These efforts might be put down to an instinct for mastery that was acting independently of whether the memory was in itself pleasurable or not. (Freud 1961: 10)

If one of the hypotheses explaining the screams of joy accompanying this game might be the revenge against his mother, whose absence makes her guilty, a better explanation is that the repetition of this act answers to an impulse of appropriation and mastery.

Later in the text Freud will return to the theme of repetition as ownership, describing it as what sometimes represents the only possibility in the analytic situation, given that, despite the patient being informed about her lost memories, since she did not actually and properly forget anything because she was never conscious of it, she cannot as a consequence be persuaded of the exactitude of what the therapist tells her. In order to stop repeating, it is thus not enough to abstractly recall, endowed with the right information passed on by the therapist, but rather it takes an operation similar to the theatrical one, that is, transfer. In this way repetition, an active staging, ceases to be a compulsion and turns out to be the cure: it could change from one's chain to one's liberation, as Deleuze thought about Nietzsche's eternal return.[2]

In point of fact, writing about Freud in *Difference and Repetition*, Deleuze himself claims that together with the idea of inertia, which remains in any case the main Freudian paradigm, it is possible to spot another model at play: that according to which the death drive transforms repetition into an archetypical, positive and affirmative transcendental instinct. In this sense, for Deleuze Freud's abandonment of the hypothesis of a real traumatic event experienced during childhood – which would be the definitive mark of a mimetic repetition, a copy beneath which something hides – in favour of phantoms of affirmation, that is, a repetition already masked and differential – already operated by Lacan as well – is crucial.

III.

The field par excellence in which it is possible to repeat the same, elevating it to the nth power, putting it to use, presenting a different point of view by a mere ostensive act, is the one of artistic representation. Here the same which gets repeated is literally so, as it is suggested by one of the most reputable ideas in the history of aesthetics, that is, the theme of *mimesis*, and yet in artistic simulation the differential element distinct from the original reproduced is already present. In cinema the ambiguity built into the idea of repetition is particularly pronounced: films can in fact be both extremely faithful to reality, thanks to the mechanical genesis of its device, and also truly autonomous, given their exhibition to the public and precisely in virtue of their capacity of accurately reproducing reality, almost creating a world in its own right. In the history of film theory, the sensational experience of attending the creation of a world of simulacra has often been stressed: since from 1896 when Maxim Gorky reacted to the screening of the Lumière Brothers' cinematograph at Nizhny Novgorod's fair, where in an article he described the spectacle as a reign of shadows, a place inhabited by spectres and ghosts, to the work by Morin, *The Cinema, Or the Imaginary Man*, which depicts the film as a double, a reflex of the world (Morin 2005).

By welcoming the Deleuzian idea of a cinema exhibiting the working of thought first in the modalities of perception, affection and action, and later manifesting itself in the impossibility of any organic thinking – with the consequent weakening of the sensory-motor relations – the psychical process of repetition understood as a mechanism of ownership displays as the direct affirmation of difference, of a difference autonomous from its model, and thus as the elevation of the false. The description of the object replaces the object itself; a falsifying narration takes the place of a plausible story; the truthful relationship and the neat distinction between the subjective and the objective points of view is transformed in a modality of the camera in which the gaze of the director is indiscernible from that of the character. What emerges in this kind of cinema is the thematisation and the direct presentation of the working difference of the power of the false as a series of forces which *gets repeated* by making reference to each other.

In this sense, the question of repetition thus understood has to do with art overall, but with cinema in particular, given the potentialities of its device – and, precisely because it is a device able to catch in unexpected ways the life of thought, many films and authors of the modern turn thematised this concept. Reprising some cinematographic examples already analysed and present in Deleuze's texts on cinema, in *The Discreet Charm of the Bourgeoisie* (1972) by Luis Buñuel, with its series of incomplete lunches, we can individuate a repetition in which the series is constituted by a succession of truthful and false acts blended together simultaneously; while in *F for Fake* by Orson Welles, which I have already commented at length (see chapter on 'Falsehood' above), we find a repetition in which the differential element is clearly at work through the thematisation of a 'series of fakeries'. However, in order to illustrate the idea of art as differential repetition inspired by both Deleuze and the psychoanalytic perspective, a good example of thematisation of repetition is the genre of the remake, and in particular two remakes of the very same film: Alfred Hitchcock's 1960 *Psycho*.

In 1998 Gus Van Sant realised a *shot by shot* remake using the same cuts and montage as the original film, but also with some important differences: the film is not in black and white, is staged in contemporaneity, and is more explicit in some sexual scenes. Furthermore, some hidden frames have been added (in the well-known shower scene, which in Hitchcock's original film is based on the storyboard drawn by Hollywood's most famous graphic designer Saul Bass, Van Sant adds the image of a stormy sky). This 1998 remake, not impressive in its results, is the closest thing to the original, and still the faithful reference to its model seems at once too similar and yet not similar enough.

The idea behind the video installation *24 Hour Psycho*, shown for the first time in Glasgow in 1993 by the Scottish artist Douglas

Gordon, represents instead a repetition which is at the same time a simple exhibition. In this work Gordon offers a version of Hitchcock's film slowed down to fit into 24 hours, with about two frames per second, rendering the images solemn and immersive through this simple operation of temporal alteration. Gordon himself characterised his work as an installation primarily aiming at an act of reappropriation rather than at a reproductive imitation. In the words of the artist, this remake represents an act of 'affiliation' aiming at putting in crisis the very ideas of the model, authorship and originality of a piece of work.

Notes

1. The third field mentioned by Deleuze is language.
2. This very wringing of the same content from what I suffer to what I embody refers to the theme of the symptom-sinthome in Lacan: the identification with one's symptom, with what is most singular in us, the embodiment and thus transformation from subjected element into the object of one's freedom. See Lacan 2005.

Simulacrum

I.

In the past few chapters I had the occasion to discuss the issues of difference, and the power of the false and of repetition in the theoretical exposition of Deleuze's thought; I now want to show how these are depicted cinematographically in the work of the Chilean director Raúl Ruiz, and in particular in a film which has at its centre precisely the idea of a repetition capable of subverting the model from its privileged position. The 1978 film *The Hypothesis of the Stolen Painting* is built exactly around the theme of the simulacrum, literally understood as phantasmagorical double, the creation of a 'world of ghosts'; the film, although not mentioned by Deleuze, is able to distil in images the 'conceptual characters' depicted in his thought.

Summarising in detail the plot of a film by Ruiz as well as explicating all its references is a bewildering experience, since each screening is characterised by the appreciation of new, unexpected details and references. It is also bewildering to take into consideration his entire production, which has been described as a corpus 'so big, ramified and alive that it resembles a *monumental universe*' (Turco 2007: 94; my translation); a sort of vegetal organism animated by an internal dynamism recalling the idea of a work of art typical of romanticism. The director himself defines the films as living beings: he writes that 'we watch them and they watch us back' (Bruno 2007: 350; my translation).

It is with such displacement and bewilderment that the spectator witnesses *The Hypothesis of the Stolen Painting*, screenplayed by Pierre Klossowski and organised in series of *tableaux vivants*, a combinatory play full of vanishing points, cross-references among paintings, but also literary and philosophical citations. The reference external to the film is in the first place to the work of Klossowski: the fantastical novel

Deleuze Studies 8.3 (2014): 383–390
DOI: 10.3366/dls.2014.0158
© Daniela Angelucci
www.euppublishing.com/dls

The Baphomet (1965), focused on the mysterious figure of Baphomet, the idol who according to the legend was adored in the Middle-Ages by the Templars; but also the earlier *Diana at Her Bath* (1956), an interpretation of the myth of Diana and Actaeon, who was eaten alive by dogs after being transformed into a deer for having observed the nudity of the divinity.

The possibility of a linear vision of the film is complicated by the interplay between the two narrators, a voice out of field and the narrator internal to the film, the collector (played by the actor Jean Rougeul) guiding us through a series of paintings of the imaginary nineteenth-century painter Tonnerre (a character created by Klossowski). The two are in constant dialogue throughout the film, alluding to some mysteries never revealed before and contradicting themselves on the number, nature and meaning of the paintings displayed. The puzzlement experienced by the spectators is an intentional result sought by the director, revealed by the recurrence of the presence of mirrors in various shots and by the interplays of luminous reflections, images and atmospheres recurring also in his other works, for example in the 1999 film on Proust's *Recherche* titled *Le Temps retrouvé*.

The challenge to recount and describe the seven living paintings at the centre of this peculiar narration, although a difficult one, should be consciously accepted and possibly met if one wants to focalise those traits in which the theme of the simulacrum emerges, the philosophical theme at the heart of most of Ruiz's cinema, but even more at the core of Klossowski's literary and pictorial production, oriented towards a reinvention of the figurative departure from imaginary and mythological subjects. Even before the credits, the film begins with a long and extended framing – a city street lined by buildings and parked cars – which seems to play an intentionally disorienting function. It in fact represents a calculated hoax arranged by the director: it seems to suggest a narration staged in contemporaneity and in a precise geographical place in which the story will take place, while immediately afterwards the spectator is conducted to an isolated internal corner of the world, free from every context, in which time and space are indeterminately suspended (the garden full of fog in which some of the living paintings are displayed during the story seems a still and protected extension of such internal environments as well).

After the credits there are two quotations, both on the theme of the body escaping death: from Victor Hugo: 'Human consciousness has expired; On the cadaver he squats, gloating, mired; Seated in triumph, he turns to crow; Each time he deals the corpses a blow'; and from

Klossowski himself: 'What do you see? What do you feel? Is it pain or is it ecstasy that keeps you afloat in space?' These are the last words pronounced by the Master Knight of the Templars to the gorgeous nude adolescent, suspended in the void, whose hanging he ordered. Minutes before the Knight spoke: 'it is a body indeed, but even if it is without life it is not a corpse', and in fact the body of the young lad will come back to life again.

While the camera frames a mirror, a dispute between the two narrators in disagreement about the number of paintings left by Tonnerre takes place: according to the collector, the paintings of the series are not six, but rather seven as, each of them being connected to the next by a detail, a gap in such a thread leads to the speculation that, as the title of the film also suggests, one of them was stolen. Before the beginning of the tour of the paintings organised by the collector we see, outside the series, the canvas of a naked boy hanged, an explicit reference to the myth of Baphomet; the series begins soon after this quick shot. The first canvas is actually the second of the series: the arrival of a knight catches off guard two Templars playing chess. The canvas has an odd detail, namely two sources of illumination (suggesting, as the narrator tells us, the idea of a world with two suns). At this point the collector reveals one of the reasons for the scandal that these paintings occasioned in the nineteenth century: the series alludes to the Ceremony (most likely the ceremonies of initiation of the Knights Templar). But, as the collector reiterates, paintings do not allude to; they rather show.

The camera goes out into the garden but before it does we have a glimpse of a dummy reproducing, or rather serving as a model for, a painting hung on the facing wall. The enigma of the first canvas presented is solved by pointing to a living painting in the garden, the first of the series of Tonnerre: the scene of Diana and Actaeon, plus a third character spying on them through a mirror reflecting a ray of light which passes through the window of the canvas previously analysed. Now we see it again as a *tableau vivant*: besides two suns, there is on the one side the light of the sun, while on the other the ray of light reflected in the mirror. In this *tableau vivant* the page witnessing the chess game is also visible. At this point the collector draws our attention to the presence of a mirror shaped as a half-moon, although remarking that this is not sheer speculation on the art of reproduction, as *what matters are the figures, the shapes*.

The mirror shaped as a half-moon returns in the third canvas, the one with the hanged boy we first saw, surrounded by many characters. Here the collector turns the electric light on, playing with the illumination by inverting light and shadow so as to concentrate attention on the figures. A mask also appears, which represents the only element we know of the stolen canvas. The fourth painting is precisely the one of the mask, but we cannot see it since, as mentioned, it has been stolen. The fifth painting is the one discarded from the 1877 exhibition due to a scandal involving some members of high society: it is a multiple painting, composed of episodes illustrating a penny dreadful about a family tormented by homosexual rivalries, ending with a suicide by hanging. Obviously we cannot determine what relates this to the preceding canvas. The narrator tells us that Tonnerre defended himself against the accusation by stating that the paintings allude to, and do not show, whereas the collector replies that they show indeed.

The sixth canvas presents the characters of the previous paintings grouped in trios. There are naked women and demons as well, whose presence is perhaps explained by the missing canvas. The movements of the characters form curves, which in turn form circles and thus spheres. The seventh canvas of the series represents a burning sphere with the figure of Baphomet at its centre, the androgynous demon venerated by the Templars, conceived as a body without soul. At this point the collector interrogates himself on the enigma of the series and on the importance of the theme of the ceremony of initiation of the Knights Templar. He thus shows the photographs, the stylised pictures of some of the anatomical models used for the paintings: in these pictures the paintings disappear and the only things left are the gestures, the bodies. The film ends with suggestive images of the collector strolling in a forest with the whole series of paintings hanging from the trees.

II.

In order to determine the atmosphere and the sensation produced by this film, which is almost without any plot and yet so complicated, I will borrow the words of Alessandro Cappabianca, who states that 'in tracing a certain profile of Ruiz it seems as if we should always be mindful of the hypothesis of a missed film (or sequence). Something is missing, and this introduces in the discourse an exciting element of chance' (Cappabianca 2007: 53; my translation). In the light of this complexity and richness of mentions and references, the spectator watching and reflecting on the film is assailed by a sort of bad conscience, according to which something seems missing, that is, 'a piece is missing', as a missing painting. However, we should stress that behind these refractions, series, combinations and multiplications there is no meta-filmic intention, no auto-reflexive approach of the camera. There is thus no speculation on representation, but simply the revelation of a world of bodies without soul, of appearances in which is displayed what is usually hidden. This is the point of the insistence of the character of the collector on the theme of showing, of disclosing, a disclosing which gets beyond reality and is able to catch the hidden and invisible part. The director himself notes this aspect in the introduction to the volume dedicated to his work: 'cinema... is the art of showing the invisible part of each thing belonging to the Creation' (Bruno 2007: 9; my translation); and continues: '[my aim] is to show the invisible demons dancing in the air and eluding the drunken eye of told realities. The unmentionable *simulacra*' (Bruno 2007: 8; my emphasis; my translation).

The theme of the double and of the simulacrum is often explicated by Ruiz in his interviews, and is above all one of the recurring themes of the thought and of the narrative and pictorial work of Klossowski, co-screenwriter of the film. As Michel Foucault writes in "*The Prose of Actaeon*", all the figures which Klossowski 'delineates and brings to life in his language are "simulacra"'. And the definitions of the simulacrum that Foucault offers right after the quoted statement immediately recall the principal themes of the film by Ruiz: 'a vain image (as opposed to reality)' – in the film the paintings, the *tableaux vivants*, the models, the bodies without soul; 'a representation of something (in which this thing delegates and manifests itself, but withdraws and in a sense conceals itself)' – the game of exchanges and refractions, and even more the mystery and vacuum of the stolen painting; 'a falsehood that causes one to take one sign for another' – a hidden enigma in the images; 'a sign of the presence of a deity (and the converse possibility of taking this sign for its opposite)' – obviously the demons, and especially the figure of the androgynous, of the Baphomet who keeps appearing in the paintings and in the story; 'the simultaneous coming of the Same and the Other (originally, to simulate meant to come together)' – that is the continuous reference from the painting to the *tableaux vivants*, a repetition, however, animated by a rift, by a difference (Foucault 1998: 127).

A few lines further on Foucault adds that we need to establish a rigorous repartition between signs and simulacra, since they do not belong to the same field of experience, although sometimes they happen to coincide. The simulacrum does not in fact fix a meaning, but is rather something that *appears* and 'it is of the order of appearance in the shattering of time' (Foucault 1998: 128). Simulacra, spirits and the bodies of the living paintings are not signs of something else, but rather they have a certain relevance of their own, in the gestures, forms and figures: the paintings, as the collector says, do not allude to, but rather show; that is, the shown paintings are not signs but rather simulacra, as one might paraphrase it. The strong analogy between the philosophical cipher of Klossowski and the thought underlying Ruiz's poetics seems thus focused around the double, the simulacrum whose nature is that of pointing to something else while at the same time revealing itself in its powerful impact as image. The result is the creation of an unfamiliar world, perplexing and yet identical to ours, in which through what Foucault calls the 'thin insinuation of the Double', the Other becomes the Same. On this point, these lines by Foucault describing Klossowski's language seem to echo the cinematographic language of the Chilean director, and of this film in particular:

> Klossowski's experience is situated . . . in a world ruled by an evil genius . . . This world would not be Heaven, or Hell, or limbo, but quite simply our world – a world, finally, that would be the same as ours except that, precisely, it is the same. In this imperceptible divergence of the same [think about the divergence between painting and *tableau vivant*], an infinite movement [the one of the camera] finds its place of emergence . . . The A = A equation is stirred by an endless internal movement that diverts each of the two terms from its own identity and refers them to each other through the action (the force, the treachery) of this divergence itself. (Foucault 1998: 126)

The description of two identical but different worlds, divided by a rift in which the movement insinuates itself, thus evokes Klossowski's language, Ruiz's films and the creative procedures proper of both thought and art suggested by Deleuze in an interplay of hopefully not too complacent references. It is Deleuze himself who in the pages of *Difference and Repetition* mentions Klossowski in this regard:

> Pierre Klossowski has clearly noted . . . [how] taken in its strict sense, eternal return, means that each thing exists only in returning, copy of an infinity of copies which allows neither original nor origin to subsist. That is why the eternal return is called 'parodic': it qualifies as simulacrum that which it causes to be (and to return). (Deleuze 1994: 66–7)

The philosophical theme of the simulacrum and of the double at play in the film, it must be repeated, does not derive from the contribution of Klossowski alone, but is completely and explicitly shared by Ruiz, who defines cinematographic images as 'instances of doubling or splitting', 'shamanic journeys mechanised by means of cinematography' (Bruno 2007: 39; my translation). The power of the double returns in its original theory of the cinematographic fruition, according to which it can be said that during the experience of vision the spectator projects another film onto the one playing on the screen: there is a double film, projected by the single spectator, overlaying the film itself, differentiating and at the same time repeating it, making the film 'palpitat[e], as if it was breathing'. We can clearly see how this process of splitting, difference and repetition of the manifestation of simulacra might become vertiginous: we project a double of the film onto the film, which is in itself a splitting of the real thanks to its mechanical genesis; in this case what the film shows us are the paintings and the double of the paintings in the *tableaux vivants*.

III.

The elaboration on doubles, simulacra and spirits is, however, in Ruiz also an exercise in concretisation, an 'actualisation of the illusory' within matter, since the vision of the transcendent there realised is a 'tactile vision', corporeal and concrete. In this sense Edoardo Bruno (2007) defines Ruiz's cinema, which seems capable of actualising and materialising all that is metaphysical, a 'materialist' cinema – in a deeper sense of materialist than how cinema has always been anyway. The evidence of this concrete character of the work of the Chilean director can be easily appreciated in the film under discussion, whose real protagonists are the *bodies* in their almost sculptural plasticity, a plasticity emerging thanks to the style and the sinuous and engaging movement of the camera. The camera shows in fact the corporeity of the various figures by moving closer to and away from them, moving around them, making them alive in their concreteness, showing them, as Ruiz himself would say, as a totality in constant outburst.

It was the painter Mark Rothko, although starting from very different (mostly technical) considerations, who defined plasticity in painting as exactly this movement in space, as the advancement and moving back determining – in the painter as well as in the spectator – almost an 'entry' into the canvas, using a line which seems to be written for this film:

> Plasticity, then, is the sensation of reality impaired to us by means of the sensation of things moving back and forth ... In painting, plasticity is achieved by a sensation of movement both into the canvas and out from the space anterior to the surface of the canvas. Actually, the painter invites the spectator to take a journey within the realm of the canvas. (Rothko 2004: 47)

Thanks to the presence of the *tableaux vivants* in *The Hypothesis of the Stolen Painting*, the camera literally insinuates into the painting, moves and surrounds the represented bodies realising what Ruiz himself in some interviews calls a tactical vision;[1] a 'looking through one's chest, through one's skin' able to show the simulacra as well as the spirits in their corporeity.

Note

1. The language is similar to the one employed by Herder (2002) in his description of the perception of sculpture and of the close vision of the statues through an eye that pats, that touches.

Sadism

I.

The protagonist of the 1932 film *The Most Dangerous Game* by Ernest Schoedsack and Irving Pichel, taken from a story by the American writer Richard Connell published in 1924, is Count Zaroff, a Russian aristocrat who owns a castle on a desert island. The count, by moving the channel lights surrounding the island, provokes shipwrecks with the goal of kidnapping the survivors and using them as human prey for his hunting, since hunting other species had begun 'to bore' him. The castaway Bob Rainsford, a famous big-game hunter just back from Sumatra where he conducted a tiger hunt expedition and author of many books and reportage on the topic, is forced to participate in the count's cruel game and to rescue himself and Eve, the only woman present on the island. The latter, who has survived a previous shipwreck together with her brother – who will be killed first by the count – is offered by Zaroff as the 'prize' for what he considers as 'outdoor chess'.

In this film there are many aspects worth noting from a historical perspective: in the first place, its germinal character and thus its modernity, that is, the fact that it has inspired and keeps inspiring various remakes thus offering various ideas for many fantasy, horror and adventure films (the latest film inspired by *The Most Dangerous Game* is *Hard Target*, directed by John Woo in 1993). Second, its evident metaphorical character, that is, its being 'a fantastical transfiguration of the fears and aspirations of an entire epoch' (Esposito 2004: 802; my translation): the disquieting atmosphere of a menacing state of nature represented by the island and the events taking place bring to the scene the fears of post-1929 America. It is also interesting that a good part of the cast acted in the film *King Kong*, directed by Merian C. Cooper and Schoedsack himself, which came out the following year (1933);

Deleuze Studies 8.3 (2014): 391–398
DOI: 10.3366/dls.2014.0159
© Daniela Angelucci
www.euppublishing.com/dls

a film that, among other things, reprises in an even more spectacular key the theme of uncertainty and the disquietudes characteristic of the time.

The aspect of the film I would like to focus on, however, is a different one, and it will emerge only after having illuminated some elements of the plot and of the construction of the characters. In the first place, it is worth underlining the *symmetrical constitution* of the two male characters, the cruel count and the castaway hero: the former is a foreigner while the latter is American, but both are hunters and devotees of the practice of big-game hunting in two symmetrical contexts. Before the shipwreck, the character of Rainsford, while still on the boat with his crew, is called into question in a discussion on the practice of hunting where he defends its legitimacy not because it is a practice necessary for survival, but rather as a sport and amusing activity. Rainsford accurately avoids responding to one of his friend's insistent questioning about the certainty of his convictions, should he have been a tiger... After the shipwreck, we find Count Zaroff entertaining his hostages–guests during an evening at the castle, explaining his passion for hunting, the pleasure of killing and the necessity, after having tried several hunting weapons in order to escape boredom, of changing species of animal. The count starts off by telling Rainsford that he could find a reasonable point of view on hunting solely in the latter's books: 'we are kindred spirits', he asserts. Thus, the two characters are presented as each being the double of the other, although diametrically opposed as regards their most exterior traits: Rainsford is portrayed by Joel McCrea, an actor who specialised in the positive role of the American hero, that is, tall, blond-haired and athletic, with a virile and clean look; Count Zaroff is portrayed by Leslie Banks, with an asymmetric face, a gloomy appearance and a scar on the forehead that the actor stresses by continuously patting it.

The second element is the *eroticism* suffusing the whole film. The female character, attractive, fragile and almost completely passive during the whole time she and Rainsford are on the run together (she also remains an observer when the actor, a few feet from her, is about to fall into a pit while fighting with one of the count's hunting dogs), is an object of conquest for both the male characters: the sexual prey of the count but also an object of love for the hero. The conquest, however, is postponed since Eve is the very prize of the game, of the match, and as such she is part of the contest, whose reward and final verdict consists in killing. As Count Zaroff says in the middle of a disquisition on the amusement of hunting: 'Kill and then love! When you have known that, you have known ecstasy.' Only when united with the pleasure of killing it is possible to experience the pleasure of sexual conquest. Eroticism and cruelty are thus part of the same system.

It being a game, a contest, it is obviously a system governed by rules, rules that the count values over everything else: the first step is that of showing the victims his room of trophies in which he preserves, with variously graphical devices for conservation, the heads of his prey. His declared intent is that of inculcating in the victim, considered as a 'player' on a par with himself, the seriousness of the game which is about to begin, a seriousness which – as is obvious even without taking Roger Caillois to figure it out – is the indispensable presupposition for the success of any game. Furthermore, the count concedes his prey some hours' advantage and the possibility of saving themselves: they will be free if they are able to survive the sunrise of the next day on the island. As we can see, and this is the third element, the cruelty of the count has nothing to do with uncontrolled violence, since hatred is also a natural instinct animated by a *lucid rationality*, cold, determined and objective. Zaroff is a 'sanguinary gentleman' who respects the forms, the rules of both hospitality and of the game, and naturally because of this his cruelty is even more terrifying.

II.

At this point, the comment by Paolo Mereghetti (2014) according to whom *The Most Dangerous Game* is 'one of the most Sadean films ever made' should not be surprising. Following Maurice Blanchot's analysis in his *Lautréamont and Sade* (Blanchot 2004), but also in the writings of Georges Bataille (Bataille 1986), Count Zaroff has all the features of Sade's 'sovereign man'. First of all, the external emblem of the title:

> Sadean humanity is essentially composed by a small number of all-powerful men, who had the will to raise themselves above laws and place themselves outside prejudice ... These extraordinary men generally belong to a privileged class: they are dukes, kings, even the pope himself ... They owe to their birth the privileges of inequality. (Blanchot 2004: 11)

There are obviously those who, although not patrician by birth, are however capable of increasing their power, because they have the power to commit a crime. Inequality is thus for Sade, and Zaroff, a fact of nature: some individuals are necessarily slaves and victims, while others are brave enough to follow their natural instincts, which are those of pleasure and egoism, of subjecting other human beings. Destruction and affirmation coincide and are natural instincts, since nature, as Sade writes in the novel *Justine*, 'is a perpetual succession of crimes' and 'does not allow for crimes to endanger its economy', thus making it inconceivable for 'the weakest [to] really offend the strongest' (Sade 2012: 62–3).

Another element explicitly present in the construction of the character of Zaroff, noticed by virtually all interpreters of Sade, is the primacy of crime over lust. In *Justine* a man argues for the reasons of the rape he just committed on his victim by saying:

> in some people lust can be generated by the very act of crime! I'll go further, and say that it is therefore the case that crime alone arouses and precipitates it, and that there is not a single pleasure in the world that it does not inflame or increase. (Sade 2012: 186)

This quotation echoes the already mentioned line by Zaroff: 'Kill and then love! When you've known that, you have known ecstasy.' In Sade, as Blanchot writes,

> crime matters more than lust, and the cold-blooded crime is valued more than the one committed in the burst of passion; but the crime committed in the rigidifying of the sensitive part, the obscure and secret crime, is the most valued of them all. (Blanchot 2004: 37–8)

The taming of the sensitive part is thus what allows the moment of suspension, in which the instinct is curbed and subordinated to crime: 'in order for passion to transform into energy it should be contained, mediated by a necessary moment of insensibility; only in this way it would reach its greatest intensity' (Blanchot 2004: 38).

In order for the sovereign men to give priority to crime over lust it is necessary to possess cold blood and self-control, what Blanchot defines as insensibility, apathy, indifference, stoicism. About her misadventures, the virtuous Justice claims: 'such is the fatal indifference that, more than anything else, characterizes the mind of the true libertine' (Sade 2012: 174). Were Count Zaroff not focused on himself and unable to experience any kind of emotion, and his attraction for Eve held and mediated by crime, he would not be a sovereign man, but rather a mediocre man satisfied by the 'average pleasures'. This is the motif that Bataille puts at the centre of the chapter dedicated to Sade in his *Erotism*, in which the supremacy of crime over passions, insensibility and apathy, are lived as the overcoming of the personal self, which seems to be extremely well suited to Zaroff's philosophy:

> These exigencies [that the crime should reach the pinnacle of crime] lie outside the individual, or at least they set a higher value on the process begun by him

but now detached from him and transcending him, than on the individual himself. De Sade cannot help bringing into play beyond personal variety an almost impersonal egotism. (Bataille 1986: 175)

Moreover, from the encounter of sexuality and rationality, blender together in their sharp coldness without the mediation of any feeling for others, there derives another recurrent theme of Sadean writings which seems in part suggested in this film as well: in the words of Moravia, 'the habit of rationalization, that is the systematic justification – of an intellectual and ideological kind – of one's sexuality' (Moravia 1976: xi). As we briefly saw earlier, the characters of Sade's novels argue, rationally explain and offer a justification of their cruelty, building a system of thought and restating their motivations with an almost obsessive frequency – especially in some of his writings. In a similar way the count, in particular in the first part of the film, digressing on his great passion for big-game hunts, is not satisfied merely with having some victims but moreover wants to convince them of the ineluctability of his behaviour as a strong man superior to average humanity.

III.

If anything, *The Most Dangerous Game* is a Sadean film in the Deleuzian interpretation offered in *Coldness and Cruelty* (1991b), a text declaring as its goal that of understanding the clinical dimension of sadism and masochism from a literary viewpoint. Sade and Sacher-Masoch were in fact for Deleuze first of all great writers, but also great clinicians, who gave their names to a perversion as doctors created the name of the illness studied. They were, even more, great anthropologists, because they individuated the features of a whole world view, of a conception of the human being, of nature and culture. The key point of the book is in fact the idea that both sadism and masochism have been too quickly merged under the concept of sadomasochism, that is, in particular, it was the vision of Masoch which suffered a 'spurious dialectical unity' with Sade. According to Deleuze, they represent instead two different clinical and literary entities, two completely independent systems between which there would be no contact (sadomasochism exists as a third variant distinct from either).

Let us for now accept the definition of the sadistic system as a separate system, literally and clinically. In the first place, as Deleuze remarks, 'a genuine sadist could never tolerate a masochistic victim' (Deleuze 1991b: 40), quoting in this respect a passage from *Justine* in which the victim of the sadistic monks explains to the protagonist how they want to be certain that their crimes lead to cries, since they would refuse whoever offers him- or herself spontaneously. On the other hand, the masochist him- or herself does not really need a truly sadistic torturer, as in a masochistic situation the latter should behave without hatred, as the heroine of Sacher-Masoch's *Die Seelenfängerin* claims about the masochist practice: 'you cause suffering out of cruelty... while I kill without mercy but also without hatred' (quoted in Deleuze 1991b: 41). Furthermore, the woman torturer should be 'trained', educated by the masochist according to his most secret design, according to his desires; but the idea of an education as well as of the contractual character of the relationship between the two protagonists of the masochist system finds no space in the sadist system.

Using these affirmations as a key to reading the film, it is clear why as a victim Rainsford meets well the count's tastes, being an expert big-game hunter capable of defending himself and far from being disposed to suffering; it is worth recalling how in the 'dangerous game' the victim is Rainsford and not Eve, the female character, who is indeed the very prize of the game; that is, she could be the victim of a sadistic game only *after* the hunting, about which the film tells us nothing. This allows us to understand the disinterest of the count for the character of Eve's brother, who during the evening at the castle immediately presents himself as a 'victim of circumstances', and who will be killed as first almost with indifference because of his weakness (a 'charming child', as the count says referring to him), and complete ignorance of the practice of hunting and of the rules of the game. However, in his analysis Deleuze is far from saying that the victim of sadism is him- or herself sadistic; rather, he claims that the victim has nothing to do with masochism, being an integral part of the sadistic situation, of the sadistic system: he or she belongs to it. Whether the victim of the sadistic game carries some masochistic traits, he or she possess them as those specific masochistic traits which constitute the counterpart, the symmetrical image of the sadism of the other, and not as masochist elements in themselves, which would be completely extraneous to the whole context. Deleuze writes:

> The victim cannot be masochistic, not merely because the libertine would be irked if she were to experience pleasure, but because the victim of the sadist belongs entirely in the world of sadism and is an integral part of the sadistic situation. In some strange way she is *the counterpart of the sadistic torturer*. (Deleuze 1991b: 41–2; my emphasis)

The idea of the double is witnessed in the novels of Sade by the figures of Justine and Juliette, the virtuous and the perverse, two young women who, although having opposite reactions to their misadventures, as sisters had the same formation and came from the same parental system. The ideas of the double and of symmetry are perhaps the most evident features of *The Most Dangerous Game*, on which the film insists with an almost didactic emphasis: the two male characters seems to be in complete opposition, the contrast of the sinister aspect of the one and the bright appearance of the other; and yet the two are bound by their passion for the 'most dangerous game'. Thus, if Zaroff is the sadist par excellence, Rainsford, the hero, is not a masochist, and yet neither is he a sadist, but rather an integral part of the game, of which he knows the rules, decided by the count and received without any major dissent, and of which he employs all the possible tricks which the count reveals without any mystery.

If thus the male characters fully participate in the game, accepting its rules, tricks, spatial limits, and escape routes, this is not a mere accident, as both become strenuous and explicit advocates of it in two symmetrical discourses: the one at the beginning of the film, by Rainsford, while the other during the evening in the castle, by the count, blunt demonstrations of the necessity of evil and the survival of the fittest. The alternation of scenes of action and cruelty with moments of sheer theorisation about the desire to kill and the ineluctable character of evil recalls the theme of lucidity and cold blood noted by readers of Sade, but even more it seems to faithfully reproduce the storyline of his novels. On the one hand, we find the detailed descriptions of the particular scene of sex and cruelty, the obscene language and the obscene details, while on the other we have pure theory, the most elevated abstraction, the philosophical justification of cruelty and of the negative. For Deleuze, this double level, as I already had the occasion to comment, represents precisely the clinical and literary character of sadism:[1]

> The imperative and descriptive factor, represents the *personal* element; it directs and describes the personal violence of the sadist as well as his individual tastes; the second and higher factor represents the *impersonal* element in sadism and identifies the impersonal violence with an Idea of pure reason, with a terrifying demonstration capable of subordinating the first element. (Deleuze 1991b: 19–20)

The vision of sadism as a self-standing situation, independent and based on its own rules, recalls the spatial idea of the limit and its overcoming present in the film in various ways. The adventure begins precisely with the violation of a limit, the one of the channel lights, a signal which should indicate the right way and which in this case should not be followed: the captain of the boat voices his doubts, since the lights seem to be in a different position than the one indicated by the maps, in an area characterised by menacing reefs and infested by sharks. Furthermore, the boat is sailing very close to an island with a sinister reputation. The owner of the boat, however, sceptical of what he calls fantasies, tells him to keep going: once the lights are passed, we witness the heralded shipwreck and the landing of the sole survivor on the sadly famous island. The hero is catapulted into a zone ruled by different regulations, beyond what is known, at the boundaries of civilisation.[2] The signals of a sinister world, different from the familiar one, are all present: in the first place the forest full of vegetation and shadows, then the castle, sadistic place par excellence, with its inhabitants – not only the count but also his uncanny servants – its disquieting position and emblems, visible already on the main entrance gates. However, once we pass through the entrance and venture beyond the boundaries we find ourselves inside yet another delimited system, the one of the sadistic game, a closed system in itself as well, represented by the confinement in the castle watched by ferocious dogs and by the island itself, a geographical space limited by the sea and by dangerous cliffs from which it is impossible to escape.

Notes

1. A personal–impersonal double level focuses on the negative and negativity, whereas masochism, by stressing the contractual and ritual element, proposes a system made by expectations, suspensions and avoidance of reality.
2. On the theme of the island, see Previti 2010.

Chance

I.

In the previous chapters I had occasion to evoke the reflection of André Bazin, the most influential post-World War II French cinematographic critic, founder of the *Cahiers du cinéma* and forefather of an interpretative line of modern cinematography in which Deleuze's thought is also inscribed. Bazin's idea of the poetics of Italian neorealist directors, to which he dedicated many essays and articles, can be well summed up in the parallel between the facts alternating as in the mechanism of a gear (the plot of classical cinema, in which each scene is replaced by the subsequent one as for the scheme of perception and action), and the images presenting to the spectator as unrelated, fragmented, each with its own narrative and aesthetic autonomy (the hesitation of the camera, the persistence on the scene of modern cinema and purely optical and sound image).

But the theoretical nucleus of Bazin's thought, that is, the constitutive relationship between cinematographic image and reality, is already in place in his 1945 seminal article 'The Ontology of the Cinematographic Image'. Those few pages, which after the death of the author in 1958 were chosen to open the comprehensive edition of his writings,[1] clearly present such a relationship not as a rhetorical, political or ingenuously idealistic device – as it has been often mistakenly portrayed – but rather as the necessary outcome of the features and possibilities of the cinematographic device capable of offering an extremely faithful reproduction of our world. Thanks to its 'mechanical genesis', cinema is configured as a 'digital imprint' of reality: the film is impressed by a trace capable of adhering to life and showing the true nature of things and human beings.

Deleuze Studies 8.3 (2014): 399–410
DOI: 10.3366/dls.2014.0160
© Daniela Angelucci
www.euppublishing.com/dls

The concrete consequence of these theoretical premises is the fact that, according to Bazin, in order to accomplish the specificity of this medium we need a film renouncing any spectacular aim, the use of studios to shoot as well as any narrative montage envisaging a fast sequence of scenes. In order to support and show the flow of our reality, sequence shots, improvisation, externals, and amateur actors should be privileged. Italian neorealism, which Bazin followed attentively since its beginnings and on which he wrote profusely, represents the incarnation of this theory. In the work of authors such as Roberto Rossellini, Vittorio De Sica and Cesare Zavattini, the fact, the 'fragment of reality', is respected in its integrity, bringing to completion the most proper nature of the cinematographic device, representing that impulse towards reality obtained by its mechanical origin. It is necessary, however, to clear the ground of any characterisation of this realism as an ingenuous one: as the most attentive interpreters of Bazin did not fail to notice, the critic underlined several times how 'every realism in art was first profoundly aesthetic' (Bazin 2005b: 25): if every form of art is fed by the contradiction according to which the illusion of reality is always the fruit of artifices, work and technique, the contact with the immanence of reality at the centre of neorealist works does not represent a stylistic transgression and a return to the rough ground of reality, but is rather the result of an artistic evolution and of an expressive progress.

In order to show the most salient features of this reality that cinema constitutively strives to represent, I shall pause for a moment on the 1945 article. The main feature of this pioneering text, which represented a milestone for an entire generation of studies in the theory of cinema, is the multidisciplinary approach of the author, who calls into play anthropology, psychoanalysis, and the history of art in order to characterise the birth of photography and cinema as part of a precise wider evolutionary course. Such a course has as its goal the reproduction of reality, which is however caught in its flow, in its unpredictable character. Bazin considers the origin of plastic arts from a psychoanalytic point of view, individuating the motif of the birth of painting and sculpture in what is defined as the 'mummy complex':

> The religion of ancient Egypt, aimed against death, saw survival as depending on the continued existence of a corporeal body. Thus, by providing a defense against the passage of time is satisfied a basic psychological need in man, for death is but the victory of time. To preserve, artificially, his bodily appearance is to snatch it from the flow of time, to stow it away neatly, so to speak, in the hold of life. (Bazin 2005a: 9)

The defence against time and death by means of the preservation of corporeal appearances, lying at the origins of the Egyptian practice of mummification, is the primary function not only of religious sculptures but of all plastic arts in general, of sculpture and painting in their attempt to snatch life from what Bazin, following Bergson, calls the 'flow of time'. With the evolution of civilisation the belief in the magical function collapses and the portrait replaces mummification: a practice which certainly does not snatch the subject from physical death but rather saves it from the spiritual one by perpetuating its memory.

Following this direction, the arrival of photography and later on cinema would represent the fulfilment of the aspiration of Western painting, which finds its roots in a psychological need to substitute the real world by its double. The consequence is that in this framework the birth of the photographic image constitutes a fundamental event for the very evolution of the plastic arts. In the midst of the nineteenth century, the invention of photography, with its essentially objective character, enabled in fact both painting and sculpture to free themselves from the obsession with resemblance, to abandon the disposition to the plausible and to realism so as to reach a new aesthetic autonomy. The burden of realism would be carried by the photographic eye, the lens substituting for the human eye, taking advantage, thanks to its automatic working, of a transference of reality from the thing to its reproduction compelling us to believe in the existence of the represented object. The birth of cinema brought this process of adhesion to reality commenced by photography to its full realisation, adding to the image of things that of their movement and flow:

> The film is no longer content to preserve the object, enshrouded as it were in an instant, as the bodies of insects are preserved intact, out of the distant past, in amber. The film delivers baroque art from its convulsive catalepsy. Now, for the first time, the image of things is likewise the image of their duration, change mummified as it were. (Bazin 2005a: 14–15)

What is shown in films is not, therefore, a simple reproduction, but the very object made eternal and free from its contingent aspects, and yet not deprived of its movement: it is, indeed, a digital imprint.

II.

One might ask, however, what is the reality about which Bazin speaks, towards which cinema seems to constitutively lean? At this point the answer should be clear: it is neither, or at least it is not only, a political and ethical reference to the comprehension of the post-war social reality, nor the fidelity to some model according to which the film should be a *mimesis*, a faithful copy. What is at stake is rather the realisation of the possibility which cinema alone carries among the various arts: namely, the restitution of time in itself, or, to use the words of the philosopher from which Bazin gets his inspiration, the return of duration. The philosopher is obviously Bergson, and the idea of life as real duration aims in the first place at defining time as an unbroken flux which creates in its continuous flow, as a non-mechanical evolution marked by novelty. Contrary to the mathematical representation we often employ, our consciousness tells us that our lived experience is a becoming, a flux which cannot be represented by the 'spatialised' time of the sciences made of discrete and homogenous instants, whose fixity is nothing but the illusion of our perception. In his 1907 *The Creative Evolution*, a text in which, paradoxically enough, cinema is used as the example of what for the philosopher is the contrary of duration – that is, the illusory movement of perception – Bergson writes: 'What is real is the continual change of form: *form is only a snapshot view of a transition*. Therefore, here again, our perception manages to solidify into discontinuous images the fluid continuity of reality' (Bergson 1944: 328; original emphasis).[2]

At a closer look, the theme of the possibility of a cinematographic restitution of time as becoming, which will be a central theme in the theory of cinema, can be usefully investigated by means of a concrete example. Going beyond the predictable reference to Italian neorealism – think, for example, about the poetics of shadowing by Cesare Zavattini, defined by Bazin as 'something like Proust in the present indicative tense' (Bazin 2005b: 7) – I shall concentrate on a cinematographic work of the 1950s to which Bazin dedicates a short piece, boldly titled *A Bergsonian Film: The Picasso Mystery*.

The cinematographic work is obviously *The Picasso Mystery* (1956), directed by the screenwriter and director Henri-Georges Clouzot, one of the protagonists of French noir cinema of the 1940s, a 'narrator of a violent and guilty world, depicted with anguish and lucidity free from any illusion, [an author] in whose heritage of naturalism is above all a declaration of moral coherence and expressive vigor' (McGilvray 2003: 74). In the film dedicated to Picasso, the director abandons the narrative and realist description as well as the reflection on evil that characterised many of his detective stories, and investigates the enigma of creativity in order to show the painter *at* work, in the literal sense of the words. In fact, thanks to a white canvas, made transparent by the lighting system, behind which is placed the camera, Clouzot, with the help of the photography of Claude Renoir, is able to record live the genesis of each painting. The painted canvas completely saturates the shot so that the spectator is able to witness the creation of the work by facing it, almost assuming the point of view of the painter without having the artist in his or her field of view. To the first strokes traced on the canvas are added, through montage, layer after layer, other strokes and colours until the composition of the completed figure is obtained. Cinema, therefore, thanks to its mechanical nature, reveals in this way the 'various paintings which lie under the canvas' – as Picasso himself says in the film – each of which, at each stage, appears as the complete and definitive one. The result is a documentary on painting in general rather than on a painter in particular: in slightly more than one hour the film shows in coloured close-ups the 'making' of a dozen paintings spaced out by some black and white scenes showing the artist in his studio.[3] Picasso, meeting the challenge of the film, improvises drawings and oil paintings and accepts the restrictions due to the length of the film, which inevitably dictates the time available.

III.

In the case of literature and theatre, Bazin pronounces in favour of an 'impure cinema' that is able to – and should – blend with other artistic expressions, with pre-existing languages, and use them for its own good, representing by now a mature autonomous art and thus ready for comparisons and exchanges. In a similar way, the encounter between cinema and painting might produce remarkable results, fecund for both. If 'The higher standard and the low cost of photography and the ease with which pictures are taken, has at last contributed to the due evaluation of painting and to establishing it unalterably in its proper place' (Bazin 2005a: 119), if, thanks to colour photography, 'painting has been able to become the most individual of arts, the most onerous, the most independent of all compromise while at the same time the most accessible' (Bazin 2005a: 119), the mechanism of cinema capable of registering movement can contribute to reveal all the secrets of painting: *The Picasso Mystery* represents a shining example of this very possibility. In the first place, thus, this film shows a configuration and modality of the alliance between the two arts, in which cinema, after having freed it from the obsession with verisimilitude and offered it a wider accessibility and independence, is once again at the service of the pictorial art.

Having claimed that cinema is capable of revealing the mechanism of painting, it is still an open question how it does so. My guess is that it does not do so as a didactical film or a documentary would, but rather – as Bazin claims at the opening of his piece on film – by simply showing it and making it visible. What is excluded a priori by the director in his way of realising the film as well as in the simple choice of its subject is the idea of conveying a message or offering an explanation. Picasso himself is not able to give a key to reading his art, as his acts are not ruled by a sequence of cause and effect, but rather, as one might put it, by a continuous series of effects (as his famous phrase 'I don't search for, I find!' reminds us, depicting him as extraneous to any attempt at research, and always in possession of the result). In this sense the meaning of the film is profoundly Bergsonian: each line painted by the artist appears as totally unexpected, because it is the creation originating from another creation, such as – as Bazin writes with a certain emphasis – 'life which generates life' (Bazin 1997: 211):

> There is not in fact any line, any patch of color which do not appear – to appear is the right word – as rigorously unpredictable. An unpredictability which supposes, conversely, the non-explanation of the composed departing from the simple. The thing is so real that the whole principle of the film as spectacle and even, more precisely, as 'suspense' resides in this delay and *perpetual surprise*. (Bazin 1997: 211; my emphasis)

If the first filmic revolution affecting art consisted in the abolition of the frame, according to which thanks to the shot the pictorial universe corresponds to the whole universe,[4] this film clearly displays the second big novelty: the possibility of exhibiting the duration of the painting as its essential part, because what lies at the centre of the film is the completion of the work as a task *in fieri*, and not as a result. What we are able to see thanks to the cinematographic mechanism and to the procedure employed by Clouzot are the intermediate states considered not as inferior realities, as steps necessary to reach the fullness of the painting, but rather as the very focus of the work. In the film Picasso himself does not consider them as sketches or simple drafts, but as paintings in themselves – they are paintings under paintings – although they are sacrificed for the overlapping painting, the one with which the painter decides to interrupt the series:

> What *The Picasso Mystery* reveals is not that creation takes a certain amount of time, which we already knew, but that duration may be an integral part of the work itself, and additional dimension, which is foolishly ignored once a painting has been completed. More accurately, all we knew until now were

'canvases', vertical sections of a creative flow more or less arbitrarily decided upon by the painter himself, in sickness and in health. What Clouzot at least reveals is the painting itself, i.e., a work that exists in time, that has its own duration, its own life, and sometimes – as at the end of the film – a death that precedes the extinction of the artist. (Bazin 1997: 212)

If the work-in-progress of painting or its transparent realisation were not new in cinemas, Clouzot, by excluding from the film any didactical, biographical or descriptive aspect, has the merit of making them the true and only spectacular elements of his work, obtaining the entire film from the vision of duration in itself. As already said, the idea that cinema is the only device able to reveal the proper temporality of painting highlights among other things an often present and essential element of Bazin's thought: namely, the conviction that the novelty of the cinematographic image brings to bear change and evolution for all other arts as well. In this case we can say that cinema complicates the traditional system of arts as it was envisioned by Lessing in the eighteenth century, making painting – paradoxically enough – a temporal art.

The will of the director to make visible the becoming beyond the forms also justifies, according to Bazin, his decision to accelerate the action, killing any idle time or showing more than one stroke at the same time. The restrictions of montage, very far from a strict prescription as has been usually understood, are eluded when, for example, the acceleration is exhibited, manifested but not used to deceive and seduce the spectator with a false combination of images: Clouzot understood the necessity of the time of the show (as opposed to that of reality) – given that *The Picasso Mystery* is a film and not a documentary – that however neither betrays nor distorts real time, Bergson's concrete duration.

In a way, in some similar aspects to Clouzot's project on Picasso, the aspiration to make duration visible, the flow of time, lies at the centre of the poetics of the contemporary artist Bill Viola. With the aid of digital composition, in his art videos Viola presents the themes of the great pictorial works of the tradition in a composition in which movement is played in slow motion. Examples of this appearance of time in person, as Deleuze would have called it, of a fourth dimension which seems to be constituted as 'thinking' and tangible in front of the spectator (almost a concretisation of the Bergsonian idea of 'the cone of memory'), are works by Viola such as *The Greeting* (1995), inspired by Pontormo's *Visitation* (1514–16), or rather *Emergence* (2002), with Christ emerging from the baptismal font in an extreme slow motion which makes the movements of the various characters fluctuate in the visual field. As the artist himself comments:

For me one of the decisive moments of the last one hundred and fifty years is the animation of the image, the advent of moving images. Perhaps one day we would acknowledge that the insertion of the time factor in visual arts has been as crucial as the affirmation of the value of perspective by Brunelleschi, opening in this way the three-dimensional space in painting. Nowadays painting has a fourth dimension, and images have acquired life... The true basic instruments, the true raw material, are not the video camera or the monitor, but rather time and experience. (Viola 2008: 191; my translation)

IV.

The unpredictable and surprising character of Picasso's painting revealed by Clouzot's films carries another element worth noticing, which, however, is barely appreciable in Bazin's writing, mentioned only in the long quotation reported in the previous paragraph without being properly developed. It is what we might call the role of *chance*, of the strange contingency guiding the pictorial gesture once we describe it not as the outcome of cause–effect relations, but rather, exactly, as the spontaneous outcome of the artistic process.

The theme of fortuitousness strongly emerges in the analysis of another great painter, namely Francis Bacon, that Gilles Deleuze sketches in his *Francis Bacon: The Logic of Sensation* (2003). His painting, whose aim is that of making visible the invisible forces operating on bodies, shifting them and deforming them, is defined as neither an abstract nor a figurative art, but rather as a 'figural' one. A figural painting is one capable of preserving the figure without becoming an illustrative or representative gesture, without implying a narration (curiously enough, this is the goal of Clouzot as well, who with *The Picasso Mystery* realises a film halfway between realism and abstraction, a film which is clearly neither narrative nor constituted by images alone, similarly to experimental avant-garde films). What might the painter do in order to overcome the pictorial character of painting without taking the road of pure abstraction, avoiding both painting clichés and subverting pictorial clichés by means of exclusively intellectual operations? Deleuze answers:

'Free marks' will have to be made rather quickly on the image being painted so as to destroy the nascent figuration in it and to give the Figure a chance, which is the *improbable itself*. These marks are accidental, 'by chance'; but clearly the same word, 'chance,' no longer designates probabilities, but now designates a type of choice or action without probability. These marks can be called 'nonrepresentative' precisely because they depend on the act of chance and express nothing regarding the visual image: they only concern the hand of the painter. (Deleuze 2003: 93–4)

However, the involuntary and casual aspects are necessarily accompanied by an element of selection that enables the free manual movements, the 'accidental' marks sketched by the painter, to be re-introduced in a cohesive and even more powerful whole.

This reading of the artistic activity of Bacon, so congenial to Deleuze's philosophy in its attention to the impersonal aspect of chance as to make one think of a stretching of his own thought, is in truth an almost literal transposition of what the painter himself claims in various interviews, and in particular in his conversations with the critic David Sylvester. Bacon insists more than once on the fortuitous character of his gestures as the only possibility of realising the operation he is most interested in: namely, 'opening the valves of sensation', 'placing a trap' to catch dynamism, arriving at a definition of himself as 'a medium of chance'. A too self-conscious and intentional practice, in fact, risks missing its mark of capturing the forces and the vital element, which can be truly seized only by 'inevitable' marks and colours driven by the odd necessity of chance (Sylvester 2003: 17, 50, 120, 84; my translation). And chance is recalled by Bacon as an always present vital force going beyond the specific moment of painting. For example, to the question on the reason why, if life is a game without any sense as he often claims, he still wants to live, he replies: 'I am avid of living, and I am avid as an artist. I am avid of what chance can, and I hope will, give me: what overtakes by far whatever can be logically calculated' (Sollers 2001: 13; my translation). This new logic obtained by illogical means, united to the avidity for life, places Bacon in the series of overflowing and extreme characters dear to Deleuze, in which Welles partakes as well, with whom the painter shares a love for Shakespeare and for the great tragic figures (as well as a bizarre form of Nietzscheism: as Bacon would say, 'my male ideal? The Nietzsche of the football team' (quoted in Sollers 2001: 44)).

From the point of view of the pictorial production, the casual, involuntary marks are 'capable of suggesting deeper ways with which trapping the fact one is obsessed with', without limiting oneself to the simple illustration of the object represented (Sylvester 2003: 50; my translation). This aspect, which aims at the destruction of any figurative eventuality, is well described by Deleuze:

These almost blind manual marks attest to the intrusion of another world into the visual world of figuration. To a certain extent, they remove the painting from the optical organization that was already reigning over it and rendering it figurative in advance. The painter's hand intervenes in order to shake its own dependence and break up the sovereign optical organization: one can no longer see anything, as if in a catastrophe, a chaos. (Deleuze 2003: 101)

But Bacon does not fail to highlight at the same time how instinct and spontaneous gestures are rooted in a certain kind of knowledge and wisdom, and should involve the establishment of a certain order if one wants to 'open up a field of sensations', if one wants to violently affect 'the nervous system' of the spectator. In this sense, as Deleuze himself notices, chance coincides with an act of choice, free and hazardous. As we can read in a 1962 interview,

> You know, in my case each painting... is something fortuitous. I foresee it in my mind, I foresee it, and yet I am almost never able to realize it as I foresaw it. It transforms when I apply the color... And color often does better than I am able to do. Is it a fortuitous fact? Perhaps one might say that that is not accidental, because choosing to preserve a part of this chance over another becomes a selective process. One obviously tries to keep the vitality of the hazard preserving the continuity. (Sylvester 2003: 16; my translation)

The burst of hazard into continuity, of chaos into order, of recklessness in knowing, belongs for Bacon in the first place to the initial phase of a work, a pre-pictorial act in which the artist might throw the colours casually onto the canvas or draw some lines without precisely knowing where he or she is driving to ('I rush my hand. Very simply I push the painting in the hand and I rush it' (Sylvester 2003: 81; my translation)); still, such a burst can take place in the middle of the work as well, when the painting can undergo some unexpected transformations leading the artist to unforeseen places, transformations instantly hitting the spectator the more so when they are accomplished almost without will. In this respect Bacon tells us how more than once, out of pure exhaustion, he covered a painting he considered trivial and too illustrative with colours and casual brush strokes, and suddenly acknowledged that those marks, intended to destroy the painting, were closer to the image he was striving to achieve. Eventually, although not explicitly acknowledged, the casual factor seems to determine the outcome as well, given that the painter, driven by a mix of unconsciousness and consciousness, takes the instinctive choice to stop his hand.

All this – and indeed this is a result only cinema is able to obtain – is clearly noticeable at work in the Picasso painting for Clouzot, although in Bazin's piece this is related to the spontaneity and novelty of the creative act, rather than to the unconscious and irrational forces to which Bacon often refers to in his conversations on painting. The relation between Bacon and Picasso, of which we find no trace in Deleuze, has on the other hand been stressed by Philippe Sollers who, by not overlooking the theme of chance, individuates in both painters a 'payback critical of the passive spirit', as well as the ability of their paintings of 'disorienting' the walls, obliging 'the whole room, the building and even the streets to show themselves in their fragile duration' (Sollers 2003: 29, 57, 57; my translation).

The casualness of Picasso's first manual gestures is evident in one of the earlier scenes of the film, which captures the genesis of a drawing departing from two marks, one horizontal and the other diagonal, traced by the painter utterly by chance, as is evident to any spectator, and then reconciled so as to form a figure. The infinite possibilities of metamorphosis of the painting in its composition appear, for example, in the scene in which the painter meets the director's challenge of finishing the painting in a brief time window, dictated by the length of film left. In one of the few lines of the film, Picasso says: 'Wait and see, I'll have a surprise for you.' He then draws some lines which initially form a flower bowl, which transforms itself under the eyes of the spectators into a fish, then suddenly turns into a rooster, and, at the last second, into a face. Thus, the decision sanctioning the completeness of the works seems to be guided by a will that is not entirely rational.

Bacon mentions precisely Picasso in answering a question by Sylvester about the possibility of a relationship between the very process of painting and the sensation accompanying the game of roulette (which the painter claims to love for its impersonality, as opposed to the personal relationship players often try to establish with other gambling games), the impression of being synchronised with the wheel and thus unable to fail. He answers: 'Here, I am sure that there is in point of fact a very strong connection. After all Picasso once remarkably said: "I don't need to gamble, as I constantly play with chance"' (Sylvester 2003: 88; my translation).

Notes

1. The collection of the vast majority of his writings was published in four volumes between 1958 and 1962 with the general title *Qu'est-ce que le cinéma?*, translated in English in the two volumes titled *What Is Cinema?*
2. The last chapter of *The Creative Evolution* is titled 'The Cinematographical Mechanism of Thought and the Mechanical Illusion'. In it, Bergson equates the illusory perception of a false movement composed by a series of homogenous

instants to the succession of cinematographic frames (see the first chapter in this volume, 'Movement').

3. Regarding the use of colour, Bazin comments on Clouzot's decision to realise the film in black and white (however impressed on a coloured film) except for the moments in which the (coloured) paintings are shown, stating that in this way Clouzot is able to reproduce the mental process according to which, by contemplating a painting, we annihilate natural reality to the advantage of the pictorial one.

4. Bazin speaks of this 'first revolution' in the chapter titled 'Painting and Cinema'.

References

Works by Deleuze

(1983) *Nietzsche and Philosophy*, London and New York: Continuum.
(1986) *Cinema 1: The Movement-Image*, London: Athlone Press.
(1989) *Cinema 2: The Time-Image*, London: Athlone Press.
(1991a) *Bergsonism*, New York: Zone Books.
(1991b) *Coldness and Cruelty*, New York: Zone Books.
(1992) *The Fold: Leibniz and the Baroque*, Minneapolis: University of Minnesota Press.
(1994) *Difference and Repetition*, New York: Columbia University Press.
(1997a) *Negotiations*, New York: Columbia University Press.
(1997b) *L'Abécédaire de Gilles Deleuze*, ed. C. Parnet, Paris: Editions de Minuit.
(1998) *Essays Critical and Clinical*, London: Verso.
(2000) *Marcel Proust & Signs*, Minneapolis: University of Minnesota Press.
(2001) *Pure Immanence: Essays on a Life*, New York: Zone Books.
(2003) *Francis Bacon: The Logic of Sensation*, London and New York: Continuum.
(2006) *Two Regimes of Madness: Texts and Interviews 1975–1995*, New York: Semiotext(e).

Works by Deleuze and Guattari

(1994) *What Is Philosophy?*, New York: Columbia University Press.

Works by Others

Angelucci, D. (2013) *Filosofia del cinema*, Rome: Carocci.
Aprà, A. (2003) 'Documentario', in *Enciclopedia del cinema*, vol. 2, Rome: Istituto della Enciclopedia Italiana, p. 368.
Badiou, A. (1999) *Deleuze: The Clamor of Being*, Minneapolis: Minnesota University Press.
Bataille, G. (1986) *Erotism: Death and Sensuality*, San Francisco: City Lights.
Bazin, A. (1992) *Orson Welles: A Critical View*, Los Angeles: Acrobat Books.
Bazin, A. (1997) *Bazin at Work*, London and New York: Routledge.
Bazin, A. (2005a) *What Is Cinema? Vol. 1*, Berkeley and Los Angeles: University of California Press.
Bazin, A. (2005b) *What Is Cinema? Vol. 2*, Berkeley and Los Angeles: University of California Press.
Bergson, H. (1944) *Creative Evolution*, New York: Random House.
Bergson, H. (1988) *Matter and Memory*, New York: Zone Books.
Bertolini, M. (2004) *Labirinti del racconto e labirinti della visione: intorno a Rapporto Confidenziale e Il Processo*, in T. D'Angela (ed.), *Nelle terre di Orson Welles*, Alessandria: Falsopiano.

Deleuze Studies 8.3 (2014): 411–413
DOI: 10.3366/dls.2014.0161
© Daniela Angelucci
www.euppublishing.com/dls

Blanchot, M. (2004) *Lautréamont and Sade*, Stanford: Stanford University Press.

Bruno, E. (ed.) (2007) *Ruiz faber*, Rome: Minimum fax.

Campari, R. (2005) *Film della memoria. Mondi perduti, ricordati e sognati*, Venice: Marsilio.

Cappabianca, A. (2007) *Raoul Ruiz o il cinema come cadavre exquis*, in E. Bruno (ed.), *Ruiz faber*, Rome: Minimum fax.

De Gaetano, R. (1996) *Il cinema secondo Gilles Deleuze*, Rome: Bulzone.

De Vincenti, G. (1993) *Il concetto di modernità nel cinema*, Parma: Pratiche.

Esposito, L. (2004) 'Ernest Schoedsack', in *Enciclopedia del cinema*, vol. 4, Rome: Istituto della Enciclopedia Italiana, p. 802.

Esposito, R. (2006) *Bios. Biopolitica e filosofia*, Turin: Einaudi.

Estrin, M. W. (ed.) (2002) *Orson Welles: Interviews*, Jackson, MS: University Press of Mississippi.

Farassino, A. (2004) *Scritti strabici. Cinema 1975–1988*, ed. G. Placerani and T. Sanguineti, Milan: Baldini e Castoldi Dalai.

Foucault, M. (1998) *Aesthetics, Method, and Epistemology: Essential Works of Foucault 1954–1984*, New York: The New Press.

Freud, S. (1958) 'Remembering, Repeating and Working-Through (Further Recommendations on the Theory of Psychoanalysis II)', 1914, in J. Strachey (ed. and trans.), *The Standard Edition of the Complete Psychological Works of Sigmund Freud*, vol. 12, London: Hogarth.

Freud, S. (1961) 'Beyond the Pleasure Principle', 1920, in J. Strachey (ed. and trans.), *The Standard Edition of the Complete Psychological Works of Sigmund Freud*, vol. 18, London: Hogarth.

Grande, M. (2003) *Il cinema della profondità di campo*, Rome: Bulzoni.

Herder, J. G. (2002) *Sculpture: Some Observations on Shape and Form from Pygmalion's Creative Dream*, Chicago: Chicago University Press.

Kierkegaard, S. (1986) *Fear and Trembling*, London: Penguin Classics.

Lacan, J. (2005) *Le Séminaire. Livre XXIII, Le sinthome*, Paris: Editions du Seuil.

McGilvray, C. (2003) 'Henri-Georges Clouzot', in *Enciclopedia del cinema*, vol. 2, Rome: Istituto della Enciclopedia Italiana, p. 74.

Mereghetti, P. (2014) *Dizionario dei film*, Milan: Baldini & Castoldi.

Moravia, A. 'Prefazione' (1976), in D. A. F. de Sade, *Opere*, Milan: Mondadori.

Morin, E. (2005) *The Cinema, Or the Imaginary Man*, Minneapolis: University of Minnesota Press.

Naremore, J. (1978) *The Magic World of Orson Welles*, Oxford: Oxford University Press.

Nepoti, R. (2004) 'Orson Welles: il cinema in prima persona', in T. D'Angela (ed.), *Nelle terre di Orson Welles*, Alessandria: Falsopiano.

Pasolini, P. P. (2005) 'Cinema of Poetry', in *Heretical Empiricism*, trans. L. K. Barnett, Washington DC: New Academia Publishing.

Previti, S. (2010) *Isole di cinema. Figure e forme dell'insularità*, Rome: Fondazione Ente dello spettacolo.

Provenzano, R. C. (1994) *Linguaggio e forme narrative del cinema*, Milan: Arcipelago.

Rancière, J. (2004) *The Politics of Aesthetics: The Distribution of the Sensible*, London and New York: Bloomsbury Press.

Rancière, J. (2006) *Film Fables*, London and New York: Bloomsbury Press.

Rancière, J. (2009) *The Future of the Image*, London and New York: Verso.

Rohmer, E. (1990) *The Taste for Beauty*, Cambridge: Cambridge University Press.

Rothko, M. (2004) *The Artist Reality: Philosophy of Art*, New Haven: Yale University Press.

Rovatti, P. A. (2001) 'Un tema percorre tutta l'opera di Bergson . . .', in G. Deleuze, *Il bergsonismo*, Turin: Einaudi.

Sade, M. de (2012) *Justine, Or the Misfortunes of Virtue*, Oxford: Oxford University Press.

Salotti, M. (2000) *Orson Welles*, Genoa: Le Mani.

Serres, M. (1968) *Le Système de Leibniz*, Paris: Presses Universitaires de France.

Sollers, P. (2001) *Les Passions de Francis Bacon*, Paris: Gallimard.

Sollers, P. (2003) *Le passioni di Francis Bacon*, Milan: Abscondita.

Sylvester, D. (2003) *Interviste a Francis Bacon*, Milan: Skira.

Turco, D. (2007) *Doppio sogno*, in E. Bruno (ed.), *Ruiz faber*, Rome: Minimum fax.

Vattimo, G. (2005) *Introduzione a Nietzsche*, Roma-Bari: Laterza.

Viola, B. (2008) 'In risposta alle domande di Jorg Zutter', in *Bill Viola. Visioni interiori, Catalogo della mostra (Roma 2008–2009)*, Rome: Giunta.

Vozza, M. (2006) *Nietzsche e il mondo degli affetti*, Turin: Ananke.

Welles, O. and P. Bogdanovich (1992) *This Is Orson Welles*, New York: Harper.

Zourabichvili, F. (2012) *Deleuze: A Philosophy of the Event*, Edinburgh: Edinburgh University Press.

Authors

Daniela Angelucci is Senior Lecturer of Aesthetics at University of Roma Tre. She studies aesthetics and philosophy of art, particularly philosophy of film. She earned her PhD at University of Palermo in 2002. Since 2003 she has collaborated assiduously on the works edited by Istituto della Enciclopedia Italiana (Treccani). Her early work is on phenomenological aesthetics and philosophy of literature. She is managing editor of the review *Lebenswelt. Aesthetics and philosophy of experience*, and member of the editorial board of *Fata Morgana. Quadrimestrale di cinema e visioni*. She is member of the editorial board of the series Estetica e critica (Quodlibet). Main publications: *Arte e Daimon* (ed.), Quodlibet, Macerata, 2002; *L'oggetto poetico*, Quodlibet, Macerata, 2004; *Estetica e cinema* (ed.), Il Mulino, Bologna, 2009; *Deleuze e i concetti del cinema*, Quodlibet, Macerata, 2012; *Filosofia del cinema*, Carocci, Roma, 2013.

Sarin Marchetti is Irish Research Council postdoctoral fellow at University College Dublin. He earned his PhD at Sapienza Università di Roma, and has been visiting scholar at Columbia University in the City of New York. His philosophical interests lie in ethics, metaphilosophy, and the history of concepts. He has a forthcoming monograph (*The Moral Philosopher: Ethics and Philosophical Critique in William James*) and three co-edited volumes (*Philosophical Revolutions*, with M. Baghramian; *The Contingency of Facts and the Objectivity of Values*, with G. Marchetti; and *Dangerous Therapies and the Confines of Ethics*, with R. del Castillo). His current main project is a study of pragmatist ethics in its dialogue with other heterodox traditions in moral philosophy. He is assistant editor of the *European Journal of Pragmatism and American Philosophy*. He is also an academic translator; in such capacity, he edited and translated several philosophical and literary texts.

Deleuze Studies 8.3 (2014): 414
DOI: 10.3366/dls.2014.0162
© Daniela Angelucci
www.euppublishing.com/dls